I
AM
A
HITMAN

I

AM

A

HITMAN

THE REAL-LIFE CONFESSIONS
OF A CONTRACT KILLER

ANONYMOUS

WELBECK

Published by Welbeck
An imprint of Welbeck Non-Fiction Limited,
part of Welbeck Publishing Group.
20 Mortimer Street,
London W1T 3JW

First published by Welbeck in 2020

A CIP catalogue record for this book is available from the British Library

ISBN
Paperback – 9781787396036
eBook – 9781787396043

Typeset by seagulls.net
Printed and bound in the UK.

10 9 8 7 6 5 4 3 2 1

www.welbeckpublishing.com

DICTIONARY DEFINITION
OF A HITMAN

A person who is paid to kill someone,
especially for a criminal or political organization.

A WORD OF WARNING

So here it is: my life as a hitman in one compact, easy-to-read book. I say that because I know that many people these days have short attention spans and some rarely even read books. Please make an exception with this one. You will not be disappointed.

But to anyone who might see this book as a training manual, I implore you not to try any of these practices at home, or anywhere else for that matter. The law is clear on this. If you take another person's life, you must pay the price.

AUTHOR'S NOTE – WITNESS PROTECTION

I made it clear to all those involved with publishing this book that if I was in any way identifiable, the lives of them, their families and even their associates would be in danger.

They persuaded me to talk openly and honestly in exchange for my real name being protected in every way possible. You could call it a literary version of the Witness Protection Programme.

That means the contents of this book are based on a 100% true story and events. But to protect the identity and privacy of those who form part of the narrative in this book, all names, dates, descriptions and places have been changed.

Now is the right time to come clean about everything, for reasons you are about to discover.

ANONYMOUS
2020

INTRODUCTION

I am a hitman.

It sounds chilling when I say it like that, but it's the truth and it's why I wanted my book to be called this. It's also a graphic reminder of what I am, which I hope will help bring my career to a close.

There's nothing romantic about being a contract killer. Death is a harsh business. There's no way to sugar-coat it, and actually it's vital that the consequences of my actions get as much coverage in this book as the jobs themselves.

No doubt some of you are not going to like what you read. But many more others, hopefully, are going to love it. There will also be those who will not know how to react once they've finished this book. But as long as I get you *all* thinking, then that's enough for me.

My advice is to try and forget everything you've always presumed about people like me. Put your feelings about the world, your fears, your prejudices and your preconceptions away for a few hours. You can judge me any way you want. No one is the same as another person. Once you acknowledge that, you can then make up your own minds after reading my entire story.

Now to the actual concept of being a hitman. I bet there are some people out there who think we're just urban myths. I was at a dinner party one time near my home in Scotland when the host insisted on going around the entire table making each of us explain what we did for a job. The guests before me were accountants, lawyers and doctors. Then the host said it was my turn. "I am a hitman," I said. The table went quiet for a few moments while everyone there waited for me to smile. When I didn't, the host said: "So what made you decide to be a hitman?" "Disposable income," I said, in a deadpan voice. The table remained deathly silent until I smiled broadly and they worked out my joke. Then the host moved on to the next guest.

Just saying those four words "I am a hitman" was risky. If I'd said them to certain people when I was at the peak of my "power", I would have ended up dead and this book would never have been written. But that's all part of my dangerous, inconsistent personality. Traffic jams and parking tickets make me really stressed. Killing another human being for money doesn't bother me in the slightest.

I think that dinner party is what set me on the road to writing this story. Admitting "in public" to who I was gave me some measure of release from the pressure of maintaining such a secretive life. It also forced me to think about the reality of what being a hitman means in the normal world.

I killed people for money over a period of more than 15 years. During that time, I encountered gangsters, politicians, billionaires and many others connected to the killing trade. I've been fortunate enough to always have managed to escape justice.

Before that dinner party, I'd always respected a person's right not to reveal their past, present or even future intentions. It's vital to move forward with your life and not worry about such things. But saying those words made me start to get some sense of perspective. So when you read this account of my life, remember this is not an *excuse* for who I am. It *is* who I am.

Millions have read books and seen movies about so-called hitmen. The one that most comes to mind is Richard Kuklinski, known as "The Iceman". He was the New York mob contract killer who decided to tell all after he was sentenced to life in prison. The Iceman opened his life up to examination *after* he'd been incarcerated, so you could say he wasn't that clever after all. He only spoke out because he had nothing to lose. I still have *everything* to lose. And I need to prove to myself that I really am walking away from this deadly career.

You're never going to know who I've killed as I always ensured my targets did not appear to have been murdered. They died in accidents, occasionally a suicide, and even more rarely from random acts that appeared to the outside world to just be street crimes. Police called them "wrong place, wrong time" murders. But, in reality, bad luck had nothing to do with how those people died.

The advantage of killing people by "accident" was that the long arm of the law never came looking for me. They didn't even know my victims had died at the hands of another human being.

I've always believed the assassination of JFK taught governments across the globe to approach the "killing game" in a different way. He was taken out by a sniper's bullet and that sparked countless conspiracy theories. But there would have been little or no speculation if he'd committed suicide or died in a road accident.

Today, Russia's hard-nosed president Vladimir Putin is the global master of the dark art of encouraging his enemies to be killed in those ways. I heard that Putin recently set up a secret squad of killers, who are trained specifically to do such dirty deeds at his behest. It is even said that they're on standby 24/7 for new missions against Russia's supposed enemies. It's lucky Putin's killer squad didn't exist when I was at my peak. I have no doubt they would have come after me.

But please don't presume this book is going to feature the gory details of each kill. I don't think it's right to gloat and I have the utmost respect for my victims' families and friends. I have no wish to rub in what happened to their loved ones.

My job is reprehensible enough without those sorts of details. If you're after a bloodfest, look elsewhere.

No, my story also includes all the same everyday shit that most people go through. My life is a precarious balancing act between at least two completely different worlds. That means there are many moments when I've faced the same problems as everyone else. I still burn the toast, break the dishwasher and forget to pay household bills.

But what a life I've led. I've travelled the world, often in private jets, enjoyed the sort of luxury lifestyle that most can only dream about, and it's all down to being a professional killer. Hence you might imagine me to be a combination of Charles Bronson in *The Mechanic* and John Cusack in *Grosse Pointe Blank*. But that's not really the case at all.

I'm so understated to look at that you probably wouldn't notice me in a bar or on a plane. I could be any one of a million other guys. That's part of the key to my success. I can slide into places without most people noticing, thanks to being middle-aged with dark curly hair and a splash of subtle grey at the sides. I could be Spanish, Italian, Jewish, Arab or just about anything other than Nordic. I consider the real me to be black, although my actual nationality is a complicated issue. But my colour is irrelevant to this story. It's what I do that counts, at the end of the day.

Killing is my business. I'm not that interested in material possessions. I was more addicted to the excitement and power it provided to me.

Ultimately, I've tried to recreate my life story as it twists and turns through the mean streets of many places, including London, New York, Los Angeles, the Costa del Sol, Bangkok, Scotland and even the largest rainforest in the world.

You could say I'm telling my story without taking any real responsibility for what I've done. In a way, that is right, but I know that unless I get everything "out there" I cannot possibly start to move on with my life. I also want this book to be like a form of therapy. I'm trying not to hide anything in the hope that telling my story will not only change me for the better, but also perhaps put off anyone tempted to follow the same path. So by deconstructing my life here, I've had to face up to certain truths about myself and how I reached this place.

Shakespeare's Macbeth perfectly summed up the way that killing other people can turn all your dreams into nightmares. He said quite simply: "I have murdered sleep." Macbeth's anxiety and subsequent nightmares about taking the life of another human being forced him to relive that killing over and over. I often wake up in the middle of the night having had macabre nightmares in which I've killed one of my victims and am about to die. But my own death never actually happens, which could be an omen of sorts.

Obviously, those nightmares are an inevitable conse-quence of what I did for a living. Those visions dominate my subconscious and will no doubt remain there for the rest of my life. And the message from those nightmares is unequivocal. There is no turning back.

PROLOGUE – THE SECRET

Stories like mine usually start with a gruesome kill. But there is a much more dramatic element that holds everything together and explains how I got to this place.

It is THE SECRET. It grew inside me from an early age. If no one knew it, I was safe. That means absolutely no one. But if it were to get out there, blood would be spilled.

I was brought up believing that keeping secrets was the key to a happy life, and it was only a long time later that I discovered that the opposite was true. I blame my mother for that. She started me off young by making me promise not to tell my father after she drunkenly smashed his car up while driving on the road that ran through the forest near our home. That secret seemed empowering and energizing for me as a child. It gave me a hold over my mother. If she didn't do what I asked, I would threaten to tell my father her secret.

So the need to have secrets has evolved inside me uninterrupted since childhood. While many hate the burden of carrying a secret, I always enjoyed it. And being a hitman is one hell of a secret! The weight of it is so heavy it could have either driven me to an early grave or ended up being exposed by someone intent on revenge.

I held on to this secret for decades. It's hard to pretend to be part of the "normal" world when you know that the real version of yourself is someone who would shock and be reviled by most people. So, the key ingredient of my entire story is how I managed to keep the biggest secret intact. I had to be prepared to kill in order to do that, though.

It certainly helped that I lived in a world few dared to enter. But in order to move on from my life as a hitman I had to go into the forest near my home to retrieve the ultimate evidence of that secret life, which had protected me for so long.

* * *

There is a starkness that comes from being alone in a forest surrounded by tall, spindly trees and a myriad of wildlife. There are no echoes there. The sounds of the forest are muffled. But inside it exists a subterranean world filled with creatures and foliage beyond most people's wildest imaginations. But I was familiar with it all. The feelings that this forest provoked inside me had been part of my life since childhood.

On this particular day, it was lightly snowing following a heavy overnight storm that had coated the trees and ground with a blanket of white. I was undertaking a journey from my home on the edge of that same forest to locate something which I'd buried close to a stream. I needed to find it and dig it up, so that I could use it as a bargaining chip to save myself and my wife.

As I trudged through soggy bracken, long shadows danced across the ground as the moon played mind-games with my head. First, I needed to find two small logs I'd earlier left leaning against a tree as a sign, but the ever-thickening snow-storm was clouding my vision.

I eventually found the logs, which would guide me further into the forest until I reached a narrow stream, which twisted and turned through the snow-covered foliage. Just then, I thought I heard someone behind me. I stopped for a moment and turned around to look, but there was no sign of anyone. In my line of business, paranoia is so pervasive that one often has to try extra hard to ignore the sort of fears that come at you every single day. Today, though, I was taking no chances, and looked again just to be sure. I couldn't see anyone. You see, it was imperative that *no one* knew where this item was hidden in that forest.

With darkness now descended, the silhouettes of the trees looked down at me eerily like crotchety old men as a strong breeze picked up. That wind shook the overhead branches of some trees, sending icy clusters of snow crashing to the ground ahead of me. I could just make out the full moon rising slowly to the east, through the parted clouds.

As I continued through the heavy overgrowth, the snow beneath my feet smelled almost sweet, provoking a lot of lifelong memories, both good and bad. Then I heard another noise close by and knew that this time someone had to be out there.

I didn't turn round, though, as I wanted whoever was there to think I hadn't heard them. So I continued on my mission with my torch illuminating a rickety plank that crossed the stream in front of me. A few moments later I was gingerly walking over it in the darkness. I turned discreetly and glanced behind me, but there didn't seem to be anything out there.

Just beyond that stream was an enormous pine tree. I walked up to it, knelt down and pulled a small hand shovel out of my backpack before looking just behind me again to make sure there was no one there. Maybe I had imagined it after all.

I started digging until I'd exposed the top of a large, black, plastic sealed container about two feet below the surface. I opened the lid and pulled out a metal box inside it, and used a small key to unlock it. Inside the box were tens of thousands of pounds in neatly stacked notes, tightly wrapped in see-through plastic. Beneath those notes, though, was something much more important. This would ensure that if anything ever happened to me, my crimes and those who commissioned them would be exposed to the world.

I'd deliberately hidden such an important secret so near to where I lived and breathed because I had faith in this forest, as it had proved over and over again since childhood that it could be trusted more than any human being.

I then heard another sound in the distance. This time, I quickly panned my torch toward where the noise came from. And that's when I saw who was following me...

ACT ONE

CASUALTY OF WAR

CHAPTER ONE
THE KILLING ZONE

The roots of my life story have grown in that forest since childhood, and I remember every visit there as if it were yesterday.

I first entered it as a child more than 50 years ago. The forest was dominated by vast Scots pines directly descended from the same distinctive trees that first arrived here following the Ice Age. These gracious, upright trees thrived on land that was either too steep, too rocky or too remote to be agriculturally useful. That helped turn it into a unique ecosystem, considered by many to be one of the few remaining wildernesses in the entire British Isles.

This forest has always made me feel it was capable of *anything*. Behind each and every tree could be a bad person waiting to ambush you. On the other hand, there might be no one for miles around. You never knew how near or how far away those people lurked.

I've thrived on such an impending sense of danger ever since I was a young child. I'm certain that *not* knowing who was out there in that forest was the key to everything that has happened to me since childhood. If you can't be sure who is there, that heightens the excitement and anticipation as well as your own acute sense of awareness. Naturally, it's something that I have held onto for most of my life.

* * *

There are no magic pills to feed children to ensure they grow up to be fine upstanding citizens, whatever that might mean. Reliving my story has forced me to focus on my childhood and the impact it had on my later life. Yet those experiences – good and bad – helped me to develop a unique awareness of how I feel about myself. As a result, I grew up to believe I was capable of doing anything I wanted. I nurtured a built-in radar which kept me safe. I learned not to trust anyone.

If I'd had a so-called "normal childhood", would I have ended up being a hitman? Who knows. Spare a thought for the young victims of neglect and abuse whose lives are scarred forever by their experiences. They deserve much more sympathy than me. To them, my words must seem so hollow.

I was lucky in that I learned from an early age to deconstruct situations. I analyzed and worked things out for myself, rather than telling people what I thought. I kept most of my thought processes internal. I knew precisely what was going on around me even as a child, and this also made me highly manipulative. I learned how to interpret facial expressions in other people, often overreacting to apparent hostility from others. I would see anger in some people's faces that simply was not there.

I tell you these things as it helps explain how I developed from being an upper-class kid into an assassin, even though my childhood is not an excuse for what I went on to become. No one wakes up and decides to kill people. It grows inside you from an early age and most people don't recognize it until it's too late, if at all.

* * *

Unfortunately, I can't explain much about my birth and early life because my parents never told me about what happened. They lived for the present rather than the past and, as a result, left me with no clue as to who I really was.

I remember at about the age of four or five experiencing fear and sadness for the first time when I lost my favourite toy in a stream. But it's only now I realize that that was what I felt. I had no real understanding of my emotions back then.

I have little doubt that my unusual childhood led to me lacking empathy, though. Behavioural experts often say that a person's inability to recognize empathy in others or to show it themselves comes from such a lack in their own childhood. Therapists claim that children like me have not properly developed what they call the "theory of mind". Trauma during childhood can lead to emotional repression, acting out, anxiety and aggression. It's not rocket science to be able to work out why.

* * *

As a former soldier, my father saw many things in plain and simple, black-and-white terms. He always made it clear he considered himself to be intellectually superior to most of his army colleagues. He'd never held high office, though, which I felt explained why he sounded rather bitter when he talked about his army superiors.

This sense of entitlement didn't affect me too much during my early years. I didn't notice much about my father's character at that time, except that he seemed a bit distant, even though I was supposed to be his beloved only son. He was never "dad" to me, always "father", and that kind of distance sums him up.

While I usually had a smile on my face when I was young, it was increasingly camouflaging a lot of hurt inside. My father was determined to mould me into a strong and tough character (more or less a mirror image of himself, although he didn't even seem to like himself).

By the time I was five or six, my mother had already become a bit of a ghost-like figure, who drifted in and out of my life. She seemed detached from everything around her and rarely said much. There were a few occasions when she read me some bedtime stories in her broken English, spoken with a harsh Portuguese accent. I could barely understand what she was saying, but she always engaged so fully with the characters that she made a lot of them come alive for me. Then she'd kiss me goodnight and I'd not see her again for what seemed like days.

Meanwhile, my father would often take entire weapons to pieces and rebuild them just for fun. He saw it as a challenge. I'll never forget the day he plonked me on his knee and encouraged me to help him clean the oily parts of two Remington shotguns he'd spread across the dining room table.

We lived in a crumbling 16-bedroom Georgian mansion that should have had a dozen staff, but my father could barely afford to pay the household bills. He'd inherited the property from his own father long before I was born.

By the time I was eight, my father was taking me to the local shooting range, where I was allowed to use weapons under strict supervision. After much practice, I was soon hitting the target with pinpoint accuracy, which irritated my father enormously.

There is no denying that, from an early age, handling and firing a gun gave me a definite feeling of superiority, even a sense of eliteness. My confidence would kick in the moment I picked up a weapon and entered the so-called "killing zone", the place from which you fire your weapon. Just knowing that I had complete control over my own destiny by firing a bullet that would hit something very, very soon was exciting. I would anticipate the thrill before I got anywhere near squeezing the trigger.

That excitement has remained vivid in my mind. I'd approach the moment of actually firing a gun and the feeling of joy would make it feel as if I was floating 10 feet off the ground. That was a buzz I'd spend the rest of my life trying to replicate.

I never forgot the golden rules, either. They included not jerking the trigger or abruptly clenching the trigger-hand, as it could make the gun go off target. I'd carefully place the pad of my index finger halfway between the tip and the first joint on the trigger with no movement. The actual squeeze of the trigger needed to be made directly toward the rear of the weapon. Any uneven pressure would shift the sight picture and cause the shot to go wide of the target.

I'd then apply slow, steady pressure until the gun was about to be fired, while at the same time being extremely careful not to slap or jerk the trigger. That's when adrenaline would start pumping through my veins, which meant I was automatically "tuning" into every sound, sight, smell and movement around me. I'd hear even the slightest noises at moments like that. Stuff that most people wouldn't even notice. When the weapon went off, there was still a chance that powder flashing at the front of the cylinder might burn me, so I would steadfastly keep my fingers away from the front of the trigger area.

I learned for the first time how important adrenaline is to your actions in life. It can send you into places you'd usually fear to tread and it can disguise real and painful injuries with its power. My father said that adrenaline could even control your thought processes at the very moment before you squeezed the trigger. It helped to sharpen up those senses, so that you were extra alert. After all, guns are killing machines. The reality of what they could do was never explained to me by my father. Guns were my way of ingratiating myself to him. Just as death would become a different kind of means to an end for me.

Looking back on it now, having all these feelings about guns already filling the inside of my young head wasn't easy to handle. It prevented me from appreciating the destructive qualities of a gun, and that "killing zone" became as normal to me as a packet of sweets was to other children.

When I was about nine or ten, a lot of people began saying that my father and I were like two peas out of the same pod. That annoyed me, since he always seemed to be putting me down. If we were so alike, he should have encouraged me more.

He would insist that being a good soldier was all about being good at self-protection. Once you were out in the field, your instincts and knowledge, in that order, were going to keep you alive. Showing your emotions was frowned upon. But what that really taught me was never to rely on anyone else. They were all capable – like my father – of rejecting you.

Maybe he was cleverly trying to ensure my survival instincts always kicked in. But it seemed a cruel way to deal with a child, who wanted so much to impress his father.

CHAPTER TWO
HOME SWEET HOME

My parents sent me to a boarding school in the north of Scotland when I was just 10 years old. I hated every minute of it.

I considered most people at that school to be a threat to my happiness, so I kept to myself. I didn't have any friends. I actually felt *more* alone around other people. That's what often happens when you are an only child. Other kids nicknamed me "the coon" because of my colour. I was the first black child to ever attend that school and I was treated like someone from outer space, but with a lot less respect. It was no big surprise that I became very distant from most of my classmates. I longed to be home, despite all my parents' faults.

My father was without doubt a strict disciplinarian; he was always trying to control my movements and the sort of people I mixed with. Today, I now realize he was just constantly trying to prepare me for life as an adult. The trouble was it felt more like bullying a lot of the time, and I soon learned not to be honest to him about my feelings. That further encouraged my growing interest in keeping secrets, as there became a lot of things that I would never tell my father about – ever.

When I was home, I never questioned my father's orders, instead going through the motions and doing entirely as I was told, but then retreating into my own secret netherworld. I would never challenge my father's opinions on things like politics and religion. I also vaguely knew he'd fought in the Spanish Civil War and the Second World War, but I never found out if he'd been injured or what battles he was involved in.

Without any brothers or sisters to talk to about what was happening, I became like a human sponge, absorbing all the information I could gather in my brain and kicking it around to myself and rarely asking anyone else's opinion about anything.

Up until the age of 11 or 12 I remained happy to play my father along so that I could get what I wanted. I even assured him I'd join the army like he had, so that he would let me sign up for the local army cadets. I needed contact with other children near where we lived. I'd finally had enough of being alone all the time.

The local cadet group was considered the perfect training ground for the armed services. This particular one was aligned to one of the Highlands' foremost fighting units, with close connections to some of the most daring missions of the previous couple of centuries. At cadets, we were trained in marksmanship, fieldcraft and military tactics. We were even taught a wide range of woodsmen skills, which were essential to survive out in the field of war for many days at a time.

On Remembrance Sunday each year, my father and I would attend the local commemorations near our home in Scotland. He'd get very stirred up by the sound of the pipers blaring out their traditional highland laments. He would use that annual event to further pressurize me into joining the army.

There was one kid at cadets who was very disparaging about this idea. His father was just as obsessed with army life as mine, but this boy was determined to defy him. I was shocked that anyone would go against their father. This same boy teased me mercilessly about being my father's "little toy soldier". So one day I punched him on the nose and he stopped ribbing me. That's when I first learned that resorting to force – either real or imaginary – is often necessary.

Back at my posh boarding school in the north of Scotland, I remained as introverted as ever. I didn't learn much and spent most of the time in my own dream world, counting down the days to when I'd get home and could go to cadets or wander off into the countryside.

I much preferred being outside to that rambling, dusty, cobweb-filled house where life wasn't much fun. I wasn't allowed to watch television, except with my parents on special occasions. We had just one set in the drawing room, and that was only ever switched on for the news.

My father controlled everything. If my mother tried to watch a soap opera it was quickly switched off. She never answered him back, and gradually I started to realize that this had been an integral part of their relationship since they'd first met.

Their lack of interest in each other no doubt led me to feel even more isolated at home, and that's when my favourite forest began to play a significant role in my childhood.

* * *

One Saturday morning when I was about 11 or 12, my father announced we were going to the forest on the edge of our estate. He said he wanted to see how my survival skills were developing. I didn't know what he meant by that but just went with the flow.

After about half an hour, he stopped his Land Rover next to a small bridge by the fields that bordered the forest. I got out of the vehicle, but when I turned around noticed he hadn't moved from behind the wheel.

"Off you go, my boy," he said almost cheerily out of the window. "See you back at home later."

He then drove off before I could say a word. It was at least eight miles from home and the icy rain was being swept into my face by strong winds. It felt like shards of glass stinging my cheeks and forehead. I was angry and confused that my own father had just abandoned me in the middle of nowhere. This would mark the beginning of my life as a free spirit, an independent person. I decided never to rely on anyone else. And as I trudged through the forest that day, I started to appreciate that it offered me more shelter and reassurance than my parents ever had.

I got home about five or six hours later in the pitch dark, drenched by rain and shivering like a leaf but too proud to even admit to my father that I'd been crying during the last mile or so.

For at least the next year, my father regularly forced me on similar exercises, and each time he increased the distance between the drop-off point and our family home. My mother never tried to stop him, although she rarely said anything to him at this stage, unless he spoke to her first.

I never found out what my mother really thought about any of this. Sometimes she looked sympathetically toward me, but that was only ever well out of my dad's range of sight and usually when she had a drink in one hand and a cigarette in the other. Looking back on it, my mother was very much the junior partner when it came to their marriage. In many ways my father treated her more like a maid that the mother of his child.

Eventually my father "generously" allowed me to use a map and a compass to try and find the quickest routes home. But during the long winter months, I still often struggled for hours, crossing deserted tracks, mushy wetlands and even shallow rivers in the dark. That was when I completely stopped being in awe of my father. He'd turned into a nasty, uncompromising figure struggling to deal with his own failings, as well as the fact that I was growing up.

When I was about 12 my mother began retreating to her bedroom most of the time and became even less involved in my childhood than she had been before.

Our dilapidated Georgian mansion was in such a bad state of disrepair that there were buckets everywhere to catch the rainwater pouring in through huge damp patches in the crumbling ceilings. Our family had always had money problems, yet my father still managed to build up a formidable gun collection that included pistols, revolvers, rifles and those two old Remington shotguns I'd helped clean as a young child. The only safety measure stopping me, aged 12, from using those weapons was a small padlock on a flimsy wooden cupboard.

Around this age, though, I noticed that my father's financial problems went from bad to worse. He'd received a small army pension and used the remains of a modest trust fund to pay for my boarding school. That money swiftly ran out and he had to take me out of school and enrol me in the local comprehensive.

I didn't exactly fit in when I first went there. I was considered a posh rich kid who lived in a "castle" by a bunch of children who were mainly from the local council estate. I survived in the early days at that school after learning as an only child to absorb what was happening around me very closely. That meant I could sense danger before it came to get me, which kept me safe much of the time.

Back home, my father's views on gun safety deteriorated the more he drank. He regularly lost the key to the gun cupboard, so it tended to be left wide open, and the only other preventative measure was the safety catch on each weapon, which I knew how to flick off.

There were many moments when I truly hated my father's guts, and having such easy access to weapons inevitably led to me thinking about how I could have taken a gun and shot dead everyone at school as well as my parents with great ease.

I had an anger inside that was building and building.

* * *

When I was 13 or 14, I went on a summer training camp with the cadets to the coast. I had a confrontation with a much older and bigger boy who spat in my face, accused me of being a "snotty rich wanker" and punched me really hard in the stomach. I didn't flinch. I'd learned not to show any emotion in those sorts of confrontational situations. That tended to stop people like my father from being even more brutal. When I didn't move, the same boy punched me again, this time even harder. Again, I showed no reaction. Unsatisfied, the older boy simply turned around and walked away. He never came near me again. I'd managed to win that battle without throwing a punch.

Similar things happened at least half a dozen times during my early teens. I wasn't particularly big, and I certainly don't consider myself to have been a bully. On the contrary, I tried to keep to myself most of the time, but some children just would not stay out of my face.

Back home I was getting increasingly resentful about my father's behaviour toward me and my mother. He still treated her like a servant, and I was dismissed as an irritation most of the time.

Despite the issues I had with my father, he did encourage me to go hunting in the forest on my own, which I enjoyed. No doubt he saw it as part of my army training. He even urged me to use his prized 12-bore shotgun to kill wildlife, often rabbits, which I'd track for hours through the dense woodland but rarely shoot. Doing this seemed much more enjoyable to me than football or rugby.

There was one time when I was alone in the forest and I crouched down in a marksman's stance to shoot a deer for the first time. I let my finger stroke the trigger for ages before tears began streaming down my cheeks. I lowered my gun, as I'd decided I couldn't kill such a beautiful creature.

It was at that moment that my father appeared out of nowhere and insisted I shoot the animal. He'd been watching me the whole time. At my refusal to kill the deer, he shouted and screamed at me and called me "a bloody cry-baby". I didn't care what he said. I just didn't like the way he'd invaded my space, as I now considered it to be *my* forest. I stomped past him as he stood there glowering at me, and this time I voluntarily walked all the way home alone. I didn't want or need his approval anymore.

Back in our enormous crumbling mansion that evening, my mother seemed even more unhappy than usual. She muttered something to my father as we were about to sit down for dinner. He exploded, and that's when I discovered he'd only come into the forest that day because he was on his way back from visiting his mistress in a nearby village. After that, my mother retreated even more to her bedroom, leaving my father to fill both parental roles – and he didn't do a good job of it.

One time we went on a weekend trip to the Isle of Arran and found ourselves on a narrow road alongside a barren beach containing huge boulder rocks where dozens of seals lay sleeping. My father stopped the Land Rover and shot two of them in front of me. I was mortified, and he laughed in my face and told me to stop being such a "wimp". Seals had actually become magical creatures in my early childhood thanks to one of my favourite bedtime stories that my mother read to me. To this day, I reckon that my father deliberately targeted those seals as he knew how much I liked them.

The terror wasn't reserved for family trips and home, though. I started freewheeling down a long hill on my bike to the local council estate at least three times a week, where I'd meet up with all the other kids from school. I was actually very jealous of those children in a twisted sort of way. I wished I'd been born there instead of in a rundown mansion filled with cobwebs and mice. One day, my dad was in town and spotted me hanging out with a bunch of my friends on the estate. He immediately ordered me in his embarrassingly plummy voice to get in his car. I refused point blank and half a dozen of my new best friends watched it all with a glint of amusement in their eyes. I tried walking away from him, but he came after me, grabbed me by the back of my neck and frogmarched me to the car.

It was during moments like this that I knew I wanted to be free to do whatever the fuck I wanted with my life.

CHAPTER THREE
INNOCENT VICTIMS

During my adolescence, I began developing a tough, uncompromising side to my personality because I wanted badly to fit in with everyone from the local housing estate. I even managed to turn myself into someone with a reputation *not* to be messed with. I told some of my friends on the housing estate that I carried a small knife on me at all times, so I could lash out at anyone who troubled me. I even encouraged (untrue) rumours that I had a small pistol hidden in one boot, which I was prepared to push up someone's nose if they upset me or my friends.

At the age of about 14, I started stealing my mother's tranquilizers and selling them to my school friends on the council estate. Unfortunately, one of my classmates eventually told his parents I was selling drugs and my father ended up having to pay this boy's father a bribe to stop him going to the police. When I found out, I beat that kid up badly, but back home my father gave me a similar beating for "shaming him". I stood there and took it all from him without responding.

Looking back on it now, I must have hated myself, as I was becoming a very destructive individual. I was distant from my parents and my teachers and any classmates at my school who didn't live on the estate.

Some of the older boys there started using me and my anger like their secret weapon, and I'd be unleashed on anyone who upset them and told to sort it out. I liked being needed.

I started drinking alcohol but stayed away from drugs completely, as that was all part of my controlling nature. Narcotics were just one step too far.

Back at home, my enormous bedroom, with its peeling paint and damp patches in the high ceiling, would become my inner sanctum. No one – not even the cleaner, when we could afford one – was allowed to enter.

My mother and father had their own ongoing problems to contend with – my mother remained in her bedroom most of the time and my father was drinking so heavily I rarely saw him sober – so no one would care as I retreated further.

* * *

Then a strange thing happened: my mother got pregnant again. It was like a bolt out of the blue and it put a smile back on her face.

Looking back on it, I think having another child was my father's way of controlling her even more, so she would remain trapped in the house. I knew nothing about my mother's background at this time, except that she originally came from Brazil.

Six months after the announcement, I welcomed a baby sister into our home. It was, without doubt, the best thing that ever happened during my childhood.

My mother managed to shake off her depression and the atmosphere in the house greatly improved, even though my father didn't much like dealing with a crying baby. But he did at least cut back on his drinking. Gradually my parents seemed to even start enjoying each other's company again. I instantly adored my little sister. She'd made such an improvement to all our lives.

One afternoon a few months after her birth, my mother asked me to watch her in her cot while she went to the kitchen to prepare supper. I played with her for a bit and she fell asleep, so I went to my bedroom and put on a record.

About an hour later I heard an ear-piercing scream from my mother. I ignored it at first as my mother often shouted and yelled if I played my music too loud. Then there was a loud bang on my bedroom door, which I knew had to be my father. I didn't answer it. Eventually, the door swung open and there he was holding my baby sister's limp body in his arms.

He didn't say anything at first but just stood there for a few seconds glaring at me. Then he shouted at me that my baby sister had caught her head between the bars in her cot and strangled herself to death. He said I would have prevented this happening if I'd been watching her as I was supposed to have been. Then he turned and walked off with her limp body still in his arms.

That evening, I waited until my father had gone downstairs and went in to see my mother. She was lying on her back staring into space. She didn't even acknowledge my presence.

I wished she'd shouted at me. At least she could have let off some steam. But with her lying there in stony silence, I didn't know what to say. I went back to my bedroom and lay on my back and stared into space in exactly the same way she'd been doing.

A few minutes later I heard her shouting at my father. "You did this. You wanted this to happen."

I then heard her sobbing at the top of the stairs near my bedroom door. I put on a record to try and drown her voice out.

She eventually stopped crying. A few minutes later, I opened the door to her room. There was no sign of her.

From the top of the stairs, I heard a car engine starting outside. I rushed to the window of my room just as her Jaguar sped off up the gravel driveway toward the main road.

I never saw her again.

* * *

My mother's clothes were found the following day neatly folded on a nearby beach where we'd often swum together when I was younger.

After she disappeared, my father accused me of causing her death. I wished he'd been the one who'd walked into the sea, not her.

I felt as if I'd killed two innocent people, but I buried those feelings deep inside me. I didn't know how to deal with them.

There was no funeral for my mother because there was no body. And my father had my baby sister buried without telling me. He didn't want to share his grief with me, whom he blamed for her death.

Sometimes I wonder if maybe my mother faked her death, so she could run off like she'd threatened to do so many times during my childhood.

* * *

About a month after my mother had gone, I went to the same strip of beach and sat exactly where her clothes had been found and tried to imagine what must have happened on the day she went for that last swim. I looked out at the view she would have had. I studied the rock formations of the cliff running along both sides of the beach. I looked as far out to sea as I could manage, wondering if she might just emerge from the water and walk back into my life.

I wanted her to let me take the blame for causing her baby's death. Obviously it was guilt, but no amount of it can ever bring someone back.

I sat there on that deserted beach for at least an hour. Then I stood up and began walking into the sea myself, fully clothed.

When I got to waist height, I stopped and let the water gently lap around me. There was complete silence, except for the sound of small waves rippling onto the beach. I walked further and further in until my head sank beneath the surface, hoping that it might enable me to get closer to her. But there was nothing there, so I came back up. Then I began swimming out to sea calling her name over and over again.

Eventually, I glanced back at the beach and saw my father standing there with his arms folded, looking straight at me with a stony expression on his face. I ignored him and continued swimming further out.

Despite wanting to continue going forever, I realized that I didn't want my father to go through any more grief, so I stopped and turned back toward the shore. Minutes later, I walked out of the water and onto the beach, picked up my towel and went straight past him without saying a word. He said and did nothing. And that told me everything I needed to know.

I still don't know to this day if she's really dead. Maybe she's with a lover enjoying life somewhere hot. I know she adored the sunshine, but she did come from a hot place, so that's no big surprise.

* * *

I hardly ever spoke about my mother again to my father. Not surprisingly, after my mother's disappearance I went rapidly off the rails and began getting into serious trouble with my friends on the council estate.

Around this time, my father and I also had three or four vicious, physical fights. We both knew that eventually one or both of us was going to get seriously hurt.

One day my father tried to mend fences with me by giving me a decommissioned sub-machine gun that he'd taken off a dead German soldier in 1945. He wanted me to hang it over my bed, but instead I pawned it for a few hundred pounds, so I could buy a new record player and some of the latest rock albums. That was the final straw for my father.

One morning he pushed an envelope under the door to my bedroom. After two hours of ignoring it, I finally decided to see what was in it.

The envelope contained one open return flight to Manaus in Brazil. I recognized the name of the city because my mother had once told me that that was where she'd grown up. Initially, I thought she must be alive and living out there, and for a few moments I felt a rush of happiness. Then I noticed a hand-written letter inside the same envelope from my father. He said my mother's father wanted me to go to Brazil and stay with him for a while. I didn't even want to leave my bedroom, so the idea of going as far as Brazil was completely beyond my comprehension.

Also in that same envelope was a postcard from the grand-father I'd never met. He said he was very upset by my mother's death and asked me to join him in Brazil. He referred to want-ing to have a close relationship with his grandson.

CHAPTER FOUR
DARKNESS FALLS

As the plane approached Manaus, I looked down from the window seat of the Boeing 727 at the vast mass of steaming jungle below that stretched in all directions beyond where the eye could see. The scenery reminded me of a gigantic version of my beloved forest back in Scotland. But then as we began our descent, I noticed a chaotic shanty town of crumbling tin shacks bordering the perimeter of the airport.

A few minutes later, I got off the plane and stepped onto the steaming tarmac. Any similarity to Scotland disappeared completely as the moist, stinging heat burned my face and bare arms. There were masses of people everywhere I looked, even as I walked into the airport terminal to show my passport. They were staring at me, sizing me up. It felt intimidating at first.

The city of Manaus lies just east of the dark Negro River, which converges with the brown, muddy Solimões River, resulting in a striking visual phenomenon called the "Meeting of the Waters". My indigenous relatives believed it to be a magical place, but when I first arrived in Brazil, I found it all weird and creepy. I soon learned that only the toughest survive in an environment where illegal sawmills and logging had thrived for more than a century. I'd arrived in the middle of the world's biggest rainforest at a time when most people did not appreciate the delicate ecological balance of climate change.

My grandfather had first arrived in South America from Latvia in war-torn Eastern Europe in 1945. As any historian will tell you, that country produced some of the most brutal Nazi sympathizers, who were recruited by the invading Germans. I never found out for sure if my grandfather was one of those sympathizers, but Brazil was rife with rumours about runaway Nazis at the time. He insisted to me that he was not one, but his backstory certainly suggested otherwise.

My grandfather had not only arrived with a new identity in South America but also insisted he was Jewish, and so became known in Manaus as "The Jew". By the time I got there in the mid-1970s, he was an elderly man in his mid-seventies, but his shifty eyes and razor-sharp wit led me to believe he could have been capable of anything. I ended up talking to him a lot more than I ever spoke to my father once I settled in Manaus.

My grandfather owned one of the biggest and most successful logging companies in that part of the rainforest, as well as an assortment of other businesses. These days you'd call him an entrepreneur.

Within minutes of meeting me at the airport, my grandfather nicknamed me "Blackie". That didn't bother me nearly as much as what they called me at that posh boarding school, though these days it would no doubt have caused an outcry.

I was 16 years old and had been parachuted into a hot, sweaty, South American cowboy town teeming with hookers and loggers.

I'd never met my grandfather before because my father had banned my mother and I from ever seeing him due to his alleged Nazi past. My father was the polar opposite, politically speaking, having fought for the communists during the Spanish Civil War and for the British Army in Europe and then Burma.

There was a lot of crime in Manaus, so my grandfather had two full-time bodyguards that took it in turns to protect him 24/7. Initially, he seemed to me like a pleasant, if eccentric, old boy with a funny accent. But that didn't last long.

Shortly after I arrived, one of his three beloved German Shepherd dogs was injured by an animal trap in the grounds of his ranch. My grandfather pulled a pistol out of his holster and handed it to me and ordered me to put the dog out of its misery. He could clearly see the reluctance in my face, but he didn't hesitate to repeat the order to kill the animal, who was writhing around on the ground. I leaned down and stroked the dog's head to comfort him, which made my grandfather even more annoyed. Then I stood up, pointed the gun down at the animal, turned and looked at my grandfather and squeezed the trigger. He smiled. I'd passed his first big test.

I would eventually discover that my grandfather was the gatekeeper for more secrets than anyone else in my family.

One day I was sitting out on the porch reading a book when an elderly indigenous woman who worked as a maid for my grandfather started dusting a table next to me. She kept smiling at me. I smiled back and got a surprise when she talked to me in broken English.

"You look just like her," she said. She told me she was my mother's mother and my grandfather had made her pregnant and kept the child and mother on at his house.

I would never have even known any of this if I hadn't gone to live in Brazil with my grandfather.

He was surprisingly easy to talk to and wanted to know all about my mother's life in Scotland. I in turn learned all about her life and family in Brazil. My grandfather even described in graphic detail how he'd "created" my mother after having sex with that indigenous woman, who now worked as a maid for him. He also told me that when my mother was a teenager, she'd worked in an illegal baby farm in the rainforest that he'd set up to provide indigenous infants to childless Western couples. He said my mother first met my father when he visited Brazil to arrange the adoption of a baby he and his first wife were planning to bring up. My mother ended up coming back to Scotland with him a few weeks later instead, and soon got pregnant. My dad divorced his first wife, married my mother and along I came.

My grandfather's openness encouraged me to share more of myself than I had ever done to anyone else throughout my entire childhood. One day I even told him about my dead sister and how it had affected my mother. My grandfather seemed surprisingly unmoved by this and told me not to bother feeling guilty. He said: "Guilt is for stupid people".

One time two Germans turned up at the house who wanted to buy a share in his logging company. That evening, I heard my grandfather talking in English in hushed tones on the phone about the two men and describing them as "suspicious" to a business associate and speculating that they might have been Nazi-hunters.

The plot thickened when I was on my own in his library and noticed some books about the Nazis neatly stacked on one specific shelf. I was just pulling one out when he walked in and told me not to touch them. On another occasion I walked into the library to find my grandfather opening a wall safe. I got a brief glimpse of some medals in the safe, including what looked like a German iron cross. But he slammed the door shut before I could ask him about them.

My grandfather was extremely careful only to tell me what he wanted me to hear. But he kept talking about my mother.

One time he asked me if she'd ever spoken much about death. I lied and said she hadn't, when she'd actually been unhealthily obsessed with death and spent a lot of time telling me during my childhood that she thought heaven had to be a better place than Scotland.

My grandfather travelled everywhere locally on horseback. His house bordered the rainforest and most of his logging crews worked within a 20-mile radius of the property. A lot of explosives were used by the loggers working for my grandfather's company. They were usually rigged to the base of trees that were so deeply embedded in the soil they were hard to remove.

Many of the loggers were men from the same indigenous tribe that my mother was half related to. One of them called Te taught me how to forage in the forest and, for the first time, I started to appreciate the significance of my mother's indigenous blood. Then one day, Te was seriously injured when some explosives went off in his hands while he was rigging a tree trunk for my grandfather. My grandfather ordered everyone to clear the area around Te, who lay mortally wounded near the base of the tree he was about to blow up. My grandfather shot Te in the forehead, killing him instantly. The other loggers then dragged Te's body away for burial.

That evening, he told me he'd had no choice but to put him out of his agony. My grandfather studied me closely as we talked about what had happened. Then he admitted very casually that Te had been my uncle. I was very upset. I'd never had a chance to talk to him about my mother when he'd been alive.

Not long after this, my grandfather and I were in a bar in Manaus when an indigenous woman rounded on him in Portuguese. She was angry about the way that my uncle Te had died and accused my grandfather of shooting him in cold blood. She also revealed that the booby trap which had mortally injured my grandfather's German Shepherd after I first arrived in Brazil had actually been set for the indigenous people I was related to through my mother. My grandfather had wanted to stop them straying onto his grounds from the nearby rainforest. My grandfather and this woman had a furious row and he pulled his pistol out and started waving it at her. I eventually calmed him down and drove him home because he was so drunk.

But despite all these incidents, I somehow felt more at home in the Brazilian rainforest than back with my father in Scotland. I didn't really fully appreciate at the time that my grandfather was making a fortune out of destroying the forests I so adored and exploiting the people I was directly descended from.

But there were some even more disturbing characters connected to my grandfather.

CHAPTER FIVE
THE DEBT

One day my grandfather introduced me to a group of Catholic priests who lived in a house he'd had specially built for them on the edge of the rainforest, close to his own home. The priests took confessions from most of my grandfather's workers and they informed him of his staff's secrets. My grandfather even openly admitted that the priests had also been involved with the baby farm that my grandfather owned when my father first met my mother although it had closed down long before my trip to Brazil. The priests were led by an elderly man with a New York accent who smoked and drank excessively. He also seemed very friendly with a number of local indigenous women, who regularly went in and out of his home.

One day my grandfather, myself and the elderly priest were all talking in the garden of the priests' house. Halfway through the meeting, my grandfather went off on horseback to attend to a problem with one of his logging crews. I carried on talking with the old priest about Scotland and my mother. He seemed to know everything about my family. He eventually produced a photo album full of pictures of my mother and the woman I now know as her mother, as well as my uncle Te, who'd been shot by my grandfather.

I was fascinated to see my mother's childhood in photos. Eventually the old priest flicked over yet another page to one that featured photos of naked men. I didn't recognize them and felt a bit awkward. I noticed the priest's breathing became more uneven and he moved closer to me while at the same time making sure the photos remained right in front of me. Then he touched my knee. I immediately jumped up just as my grandfather appeared at the garden fence on horseback. His eyes narrowed at us. He knew something was happening but said nothing.

The following day I was out on my own near the chapel next to the same house when the old priest appeared and insisted I attend confession. I'd been indoctrinated in Catholicism by my mother in Scotland, so I agreed and entered the confessional box. That same old priest's voice through the grill sounded surreal as he encouraged me to confess my sins. His breathing was even more uneven than it had been the previous day, and I walked out of the box without finishing the confession and ran from the house.

When I got back to the main house that evening, my grandfather asked me what was wrong and I told him everything. He listened avidly and never once attempted to suggest I might have got it wrong.

A few days later, the same old priest fell into a river and drowned. Locals said it was an accident but after his funeral my grandfather told me that he'd had him killed for what he'd done to me. I was shocked because I wasn't even sure he'd actually tried to abuse me.

I now realize that my grandfather used that old priest's death to try and form an even closer relationship with me. He said he'd always protect me come what may. I was too young to appreciate what that really meant.

My grandfather was all about the power of life and death and he had it in the palm of his hands in Brazil. All that changed, though, the day he was thrown from his horse and very seriously injured. As he didn't get on well with his children from his first marriage, I was the only relative who even bothered to see him in hospital. The day I visited him was a day I would never forget.

* * *

"*Nada pela boca*"

I'd picked up quite a lot of Portuguese in Brazil, but I had no idea what the sign meant which was hanging on the end of my grandfather's hospital bed. It actually meant "nil by mouth", and my grandfather had left very strict instructions that if anything happened to him, he did not want to be revived.

I was very upset and confused by this after a nurse explained it to me. He'd become the centre of my life and I certainly felt closer to him than my own father. I couldn't understand why he wouldn't want to live. So when I held his hand and his eyes flickered open, I was delighted.

I looked down at the sinister gap between his two front teeth as he lay there flat on his back, sweating profusely. My mother and I had the same gap and an image of her kept popping in and out of my head. I managed to smile down at him as he lay there.

"Come here, Blackie," he whispered to me. He grabbed my wrist surprisingly tightly. "Listen," he whispered hoarsely, in his distinct Eastern European accent. His clammy, bony hand squeezed my wrist even tighter. "You remember the priest?"

I nodded. I'd never forgotten how I'd signed that poor old bastard's death sentence.

"Now you do something for me," he whispered, the yellowing, bloodshot whites of his eyes contrasting sharply with his bluey-grey pupils as he focused on me. His hand remained clamped around my wrist, but it was starting to weaken. "It's time, Blackie," he muttered. His eyes closed moments later for the last time.

How dare he abandon me, I thought to myself. I'd almost learned to trust another human being and he had gone. I'd never make that mistake again.

I learned a lot about myself from that stay with my grandfather and, in his own weird, twisted way, he's guided me through life ever since.

* * *

After my grandfather died, the adult children from his earlier marriage planned to take over his logging company and made it clear they wanted me out and that I had no right to any part of his estate.

I arrived back in Scotland, a very confused teenager about to celebrate my eighteenth birthday, who'd already experienced more than his fair share of death and destruction.

My father was as distant as ever but seemed even more bitter about the death of my mother and baby sister. It must have been painful for him. I reminded him so much of what had happened. But I did confront him about why he'd never allowed my mother and I to see my grandfather. He actually admitted to me that he had no actual proof my grandfather had even been a Nazi. He just didn't like him, which I found even more hurtful. He admitted a lot of this was down to his family actually being Jewish, although they'd hidden it when they immigrated to Scotland in the late 1800s. They'd changed their name to make it sound more Scottish and eventually made a fortune from the cotton industry.

My father and I tried to avoid each other a lot after that. I knew he wanted me to join the army and leave him in peace. I was determined to do exactly what I wanted, and when I was ready I would get as far away from my father as possible. I had a plan which I knew he'd disapprove of, but I didn't give a fuck what he thought.

CHAPTER SIX
ON THE FRONT LINE

The French Foreign Legion is a military service branch of the French Army established in 1831. Legionnaires are highly trained infantry soldiers and the Legion is unique in that it is open to foreign recruits. One of the biggest incentives I had to join the Legion rather than the British Army was that it was based in Algeria, which was far enough away from my father for me to never have to deal with him again. He didn't even know I'd joined the Legion until I sent him a postcard from North Africa.

The Legion was perfect for me. The language barrier didn't seem to matter and everyone who'd enrolled shared a common obsession with running away from something. The first six months consisted of gruelling training, much of it out in the Sahara Desert. It still felt good, as I was fully free of my father. Sure, it was tough, and there were some officers who enjoyed bullying us. But after Brazil, I could handle just about anything. Guns, violence and death were already part of life for me. A lot of the other kids who joined the Legion struggled in comparison. As a result, many of them soon fell by the wayside.

I eventually found myself under a half British, half French commanding officer with a shady past. He'd served in Northern Ireland with the British Army and left under a cloud, though none of us knew what he'd actually done. At first, he seemed typical of the type of British army officer I thought I'd managed to avoid by not joining the regular services. He had an unruly mop of blonde hair and a plummy, nasal accent that made him sound like a gritty version of Kenneth Williams.

He sent us on punishing training exercises in the desert and was constantly on my back about something or other. Gradually, he did begin to take the time to ask us all questions about ourselves, and he seemed to have a genuine interest in who we were as human beings. I eventually came to appreciate his honesty, loyalty and gallows humour. In any case, I was perhaps in need of a father figure at that time.

It was the early 1980s and Lebanon was in the grip of a vicious, bloody civil war, and units of French troops – including some from the Legion – were sent to Beirut by the French government to help the Americans try and find a peaceful solution. We landed in Beirut from a French warship anchored off the coast in the dead of night after boarding a troop vessel in Larnaca, Cyprus, the previous day. I was in an undercover unit specifically trained to seek out and kill as many insurgents as we could find.

I owe a lot to the military for how I ended up as a hitman. If I hadn't been in the services, maybe I wouldn't have found it so easy to kill in the first place.

* * *

A few days after we got to Beirut I was out on patrol on the narrow dusty streets of a tightly packed village in the mountainous Chouf district when a sniper with a telescopic lens was panning around looking for foreign troops to target. The local militia wanted a big scalp to try and drive the foreign "invaders" away and convince them they were never going to beat the locals, come hell or high water.

As I patrolled the alleyways that day, little did I know that that same telescopic lens was following my every step from a vantage point in the third floor window of a nearby low-rise apartment block. The insurgent sniper squeezed the trigger once he had me directly in his sights for what he presumed would be an easy kill. There was a brief, sharp hissing noise of air escaping from the rifle and I ducked instinctively.

They say bullets from rifles like the one used that afternoon travel at between 1,600 and 2,000 miles per hour. It tore over the shoulder of my flak jacket and embedded itself in a wall next to me. I went into immediate adrenaline mode and ducked down before turning to where I knew that bullet must have come from. Once I'd focused on that spot in my mind, I set off on a mission to find the sniper. I was soon smashing over dustbins and pushing mothers and their children out of the way as I weaved toward that spot through a maze of alleyways.

Up in the low-rise apartment, the insurgent sniper was hurriedly packing up his weapon, knowing full well that dozens of bloodthirsty legionnaires would soon be knocking down his front door. When I got to the block of flats where I was sure the bullet had come from, I headed for the stairs and began climbing them two steps at a time. That's when I caught a glimpse of him scrambling down the same stairway toward me. I shot an entire round up the stairs before the sniper had even had time to point his weapon down in my direction from the stairwell.

I waited with my back to the wall on the stairway to see if he fired back. I could hear groaning but nothing else. I eventually moved tentatively up the steps to where I could see the sniper's limp arm hanging over the edge of a step. As I carefully moved further up the stairs, his body gradually came into view. There was also a child lying dead on the floor just behind him.

Below me, I heard the voice of other legionnaires shouting up at me to see if I was okay. I acknowledged I was safe, but my voice was very wobbly as I was transfixed by the body of that child just a few feet away. Then I heard my CO ordering other legionnaires to spread out around the neighbourhood because another sniper was on the run. He shouted up at me that he was coming up. I was so shocked by that dead child that I didn't even acknowledge him.

When he got to where I was standing, he knew immediately what had happened. He told me to make sure no one came up or down the stairway. Then he leaned down and pulled the body of the dead child closer to the insurgent. I was confused but didn't dare question what he was doing. He removed a grenade from the dead sniper's belt, knelt down on one knee, pulled out the pin and rolled it between both bodies. Then he leapt over the bannisters of the stairs and yelled at me to get down on the floor.

That explosion rocked the hallway area where the two bodies lay and blew a big hole in the side of the apartment block. Moments later my CO and I re-emerged back into the sunlight where he radioed to base that a sniper had blown himself up with a child he'd taken hostage. We both knew there wouldn't be any forensic examinations of those two corpses.

Everyone back at base later that same day was more interested in how I'd managed to run a quarter of a mile through hostile streets and climb three storeys in pursuit of one lone sniper. No one even mentioned the child, although I was struggling to get his face out of my mind. I've never really stopped thinking about him ever since.

* * *

Then came another incident, this time right in the heart of war-torn Beirut. We were stationed in the nine-storey Drakkar building – a few kilometres from where many American soldiers were also based – when a truck bomb was driven into our building.

The force of the explosion sent me flying into the air as windows smashed and rattled throughout the building. I must have slid for about 10 metres toward the back of the large mess room we'd been in at the time. I lay there for a few moments completely stunned as clouds of dust enveloped the room.

My adrenaline kicked in once again, and so strongly that I didn't even realize that I was injured. Crouching low, I scrambled across the rubble-strewn floor of the wrecked mess room to check on my colleagues.

The first man I found, who had been standing alongside me just a few moments earlier before the explosion, was now lying in a corner of the room. I bent down and began trying to lift him into a more comfortable position. I noticed he seemed very light and then realized that the bottom half of his body had been completely blown away. He died in my arms seconds later.

My commanding officer lay nearby with metal shrapnel sticking out of his head. I administered first aid to him and talked to him to stop him losing consciousness while we waited for a helicopter. As I stemmed the bleeding from the open wound in his head, I could see right inside his brain. He began falling in and out of consciousness. Fortunately, medics quickly appeared and whisked us both into a waiting helicopter.

I ended up with my commanding officer and other survivors in a makeshift hospital back in Cyprus. My injuries had been a lot worse than I had thought at the time of the attack. Surgeons eventually removed a two-inch long piece of shrapnel from my hip. I went on to have a plate inserted to hold the remains of my hip in place. But I was a lot luckier than my CO.

Those pieces of metal which had embedded in his head had been virtually as lethal as bullets. Most of them were eventually removed by a surgeon, but the CO lost the use of one arm, as well as having the left side of his brain impacted by razor-sharp pieces of flying glass. It didn't affect his mental abilities, but it did leave him with constant headaches and slightly slurred speech.

In hospital my CO and I spent weeks talking about every aspect of our lives. One day he reminded me of when that child died in the stairway and how I'd hesitated to cover up the killing initially. I tried to explain to him that I felt uncomfortable about what we'd done. His face hardened and he said it would have been grossly disloyal if I hadn't covered it up. Dozens of soldiers would have died at the hands of the insurgents if they'd known I'd shot dead a child. He admitted he'd experienced this type of covert action before on the streets of Belfast when he'd been in the British Army. He said he'd been kicked out after shooting an IRA man at close range in the head and presuming his own commanding officer would help cover it up for him. "I'll never make that mistake again," he told me.

A few weeks later, we reported back to base knowing full well that our injuries were so serious our careers in the Foreign Legion were over. As we packed to leave, my CO pulled a flask of whiskey out of his back pocket and poured us each a dram. Then he gave me a card with his contact details. "Call me if you're ever in London. You never know what life has in store for you."

If only I'd realized the full implications of what he meant by that last remark.

CHAPTER SEVEN
LOST

Back in Scotland with no job, my relationship with my father got even worse. He was totally unsympathetic toward me and said I wouldn't have been injured if I'd joined the British Army like he'd wanted me to. And the spectre of my mum and baby sister hung over the house constantly.

One day my father and I had yet another vicious fist fight and we had to be pulled apart by his latest young girlfriend, who'd just moved into the house. The next day he wrote me a note banishing me from the main house and ordering me to move into an isolated log cabin on the edge of the big forest on the east of the estate. I was delighted. I'd always wanted to live there anyway.

I call it a cabin, but it was more like a classic American-style house with a porch, two bedrooms, an open-plan living area and the entire forest as my garden. I soon started using all the foraging skills my uncle had taught me in Manaus and began to appreciate a different side to the forest from when I was younger. I no longer wanted to eat or harm animals, so I didn't use my uncle's tracking skills, but they'd eventually come in handy.

While I tried to settle into my solitary new life in the cabin, my experiences in Lebanon plus the death of my mother and baby sister were never far away.

Eventually, my father tried to make amends and started inviting me up to the main house for the occasional meal. It was still awkward between us, but at least we both made an effort to be civilized, and his girlfriend tried her hardest to get us to bond, though it wasn't easy.

One day my father invited me to go to London with him to attend his regimental dinner. The evening turned into a disaster when I had a fight with a drunken ex-officer on our table, who kept making disparaging remarks about the Legion. We ended up outside in the street smashing each other to pieces. My father said he was ashamed of me after that fight and we travelled separately back up to Scotland.

Returning to the cabin that night, a wave of hopeless despondency came over me. I'd suffered from bouts of depression since childhood but learned to keep them hidden from others, especially while I was in the Legion. Now a combination of those experiences in Lebanon and my father's attitude toward me, which seemed not to have changed much over the years, had sent me crashing into what today would be called post-traumatic stress, although nobody recognized it as that back then.

A few days after I got back from London, I was woken up one morning by the sound of someone kicking hard on the front door over and over again. Two men were standing there, and I knew instantly they were police officers. They told me that I was alleged to have assaulted a man at the regimental dinner and that they were going to escort me all the way down to a London police station to be formally charged.

In London, I was allowed one call, so I phoned my old commanding officer – the only person I could think of who might help me. He provided me with a lawyer, and I was bailed to reappear at the same London police station 28 days later while police continued their enquiries into the allegations.

My CO picked me up from the police station in his Toyota Landcruiser. The first thing I noticed was that he was only able to drive the car with one hand using a knob screwed onto the steering wheel. He actually managed to roll a joint as we drove through the trafficky streets as well as drive. He'd certainly changed a bit. He said he could get me some protection work through one of his ex-army contacts. But he told me that first I needed to return to Scotland and "sort out all your shit".

He was right. I needed to get rid of the black cloud hanging over me. Back in Scotland, I tried to contact my father. He wouldn't answer the door to me, so I left a message on his telephone answering machine. Within minutes, I got an officious call from his lawyers stating in no uncertain terms that if I ever tried to contact him directly again, an injunction would be served on me "in addition to the matters now being dealt with by the police".

The police in London eventually dropped all the charges against me but by that time the real damage had already been done. I had nothing left. It felt like I'd already come full circle in life. I was back in Scotland, scarred both emotionally and physically, and I couldn't see any light at the end of the tunnel.

* * *

For the following few months, I went into a complete lockdown at the cabin. I didn't see or talk to anyone. My depression worsened and much of it centred around that child I'd killed in the Lebanon. I had no idea how to deal with it.

Eventually – in an effort to break out from my self-imposed isolation – I re-connected with some members of the local rich set, who came from some of the land-owning families who knew my father. Most of these characters were living on large trust funds, but a couple of them had aspirations to move to Hollywood and become movie producers. They persuaded me to travel to California with them. I had nothing to lose, so I locked the cabin up and set off for Los Angeles.

I ended up spending months sleeping on a sofa in an enormous house on Laurel Canyon, right in the heart of Hollywood, that was being rented by a Lord's son from the Highlands.

Being a movie producer in Hollywood didn't require any proper experience in the film industry, just a good ability to talk the talk and access to some potential investors. While it was nice, I still felt like a walking tinder box. Some of the so-called Hollywood "players" I met made it clear I wasn't the "right type" to work in La La Land. I had a limp and a plastic hip after being blown up in Beirut, so I wasn't exactly a perfect specimen. And I wasn't interested in sticking my nose in a bag of cocaine, either. I was getting frustrated with LA, but the last straw for me came unexpectedly one night.

I was staying as usual at the house in Laurel Canyon when a vagrant tried to break in through a ground floor bedroom in the middle of the night. I ended up in a scuffle with this man and my host pulled out a gun and blasted the poor fellow to pieces. The LA cops who attended the scene were perfectly nice about it all, but for me, that shooting brought back all my worst memories from the Lebanon. I wasn't comfortable with a man being murdered just because he tried to break into a house, and the sound of bullets being fired had shaken me to the core.

A couple of weeks later I headed back to Scotland. I felt as if my life was going backwards.

ACT TWO

THE BUSINESS OF DEATH

CHAPTER EIGHT
THE "H" GAME

This time I went completely off grid at the cabin in Scotland. I didn't see anyone for almost a year. It wasn't a good way to deal with the past. I foraged a lot off the forest and had a small allowance that my father put in my bank account once a month just to make sure I stayed away from him.

One day a familiar-looking car turned up outside the cabin. It was my old CO, a man I always knew as H. I couldn't understand why he'd driven hundreds of miles from London to see me. He explained he'd just moved into a rented cottage about 40 miles from the cabin. Within minutes, H had even proudly told me he'd found himself a good local hash supplier.

I'd originally been a bit unnerved when H turned up, as I had no idea why he had suddenly reappeared in my life. But, later that day, he explained that his wife had died and he'd wanted to get away from London, which was fair enough. H candidly admitted to me that he'd felt obliged to nurse her through the last year of her life single-handedly "because she put up with a hell of a lot of shit from me".

I now think that H only told me all this in order to try and find out what was happening in my own life. It worked, as I then opened up to H about my poor relationship with my father and how I got here. I even said something that I would later regret about how I hoped I'd find someone as special as his wife had so clearly been to him.

H nodded his head and half smiled when I made that remark and tried to look touched. But a cold grimace came across his face and I realized this wasn't a courtesy call. H mentioned that stairway in the Lebanon and asked me if I'd moved on from it. I lied and said yes. He smiled and said he didn't believe me.

H told me some old ex-army contacts had come to him with a "special job" located in Brazil. He thought of me because he remembered all my Brazilian connections, which I'd told him about when we were in hospital together. But before he went into the details, he insisted on fully explaining to me how he'd killed people on behalf of the British Army in Belfast and told me more about how he'd been kicked out of the army for shooting an IRA man in the head. He'd mentioned a bit of this when we were in hospital together but not in so much detail.

H said he'd loved being in what he called the "killing game" but getting seriously injured had left him, also in his words, "a fucking cabbage". He even cracked a joke about how he could smell his insides thanks to the colostomy bag he'd had since Beirut. He explained how he'd thrown himself into a new business venture. He clearly needed a challenge that would make him feel more alive.

H sat in my garden that afternoon with a spliff in one hand and a straight scotch in the other. This was now clearly the "medicine" that kept him going. As that afternoon progressed, H referred back to his experiences out in the field and how we'd learned to deal with death all around us in the Lebanon. He started to suggest I do something that he'd once done himself. Though he never said the actual words "hitman" or "contract killer", he didn't need to. I just said at one point, "I'm in." That was it. I didn't need to say any more.

He explained that his "killing game" involved making deaths look like accidents or suicide, which would prevent awkward questions being asked. I saw the benefits in the approach, as guns were not my thing anymore. We went into more depth about the methods for making deaths look like accidents. H told me there were eye drops containing a chemical that could kill within two minutes and that left no trace in the body. We talked about how falling is the most common way for people to die at home. He said his own personal favourite was getting someone to fall off a cliff edge or be knocked down by a car.

H said that if I was serious, he would advise I start a "genuine" business to run alongside this one. It needed to be something that would enable me to travel the world legitimately, while actually carrying out commissions through H. We also agreed that day there would never be any collateral damage. Every job would be carried out with almost scientific precision. And there would always be a body to prove it. The way my mother disappeared into thin air still had a profound effect on me, so I didn't want anyone else to have to go through that.

We discussed the overall implications of me becoming a hitman and how there had to be certain other golden rules. No children or women. No cops or figures in authority like judges, as the long arm of the law would try extra hard to solve such crimes. No emotional, love-charged jobs either. This was strictly criminals or corporations and suchlike. We would leave the angry wives and husbands hiring hitmen market to others.

The key to our survival would be that we should be the only ones who knew about the jobs themselves. I wouldn't even tell him any of the details of how a job would actually be carried out. That way he'd never have any evidence to tie me to a death. I did it as much for his protection, as well as my own. I knew that if H was ever compromised, he'd be a threat to my security, and vice versa. We also agreed that no one else should be involved in actual kills because that would constitute a security risk, as it would mean there would be witnesses to what had occurred.

A 50/50 split on all jobs seemed sensible. That might, to many people, seem a little unfair on me, but I realized that unless we shared everything it would all end in tears, probably much worse than that. The minimum fee would be £100,000, although H said he hoped most fees would be considerably more than that. H would be the marketing man, the salesman and the co-chairman, and I would do what he called "the dirty work".

It was the first time since my grandfather that I felt in tune with another human being. We'd originally connected through the secret of that boy's death on the stairway, but I felt that this would elevate our relationship to another level.

H had already taught me the meaning of the word loyal, which was something my parents never once managed. I knew that his inimitable free spirit meant no one could ever pressure him to do something he didn't want to do, as he didn't give a toss. He didn't care who was rich and who was poor. In his twisted world, people were all equal, and I respected that.

By the end of our discussion that day I was ready to take on that first job in Brazil. At first, I wasn't entirely sure what motivation was driving me forward. It certainly wasn't just money, even though I knew we could earn some mouth-watering sums. Looking back on it, I think my overriding feeling was that I had nothing to lose.

Then H revealed the identity of my first intended target.

CHAPTER NINE
AN EYE FOR AN EYE

Settling a score was never my primary motivation for taking that first job, but when H told me who my target was, I knew it would be particularly satisfying. He was my grandfather's oldest son, who, in effect, was my step-uncle.

Looking back on it now, H no doubt knew this would increase the likelihood of me doing it, but I didn't really care. I wanted to do that job in order to move on with my life. I also needed the money. And H promised me that no future job would cross over with my personal life.

My step-uncle and his two sisters had been really nasty to me after my grandfather died and pushed me out of Brazil to make sure I didn't make any claim on their inheritance. Now – many years later – that same step-uncle was trying to ruin a lucrative takeover of my grandfather's business and it was about to cost him his life.

The job itself came through a large Brazilian corporation who wanted to expand their own logging business. My step-uncle was refusing to sell my grandfather's business to them unless they paid an extortionate price. This corporation had lots of friends in high places in Brazil, including politicians and other rival businessmen. They all wanted my step-uncle out of the way. This meant I had to make doubly sure he did not know I was in any way responsible.

I also knew only too well that my grandfather hated his oldest son. He'd sided with my grandfather's first wife – his mother – when their marriage fell apart after they first arrived in Brazil. As a result, my grandfather had criticized him constantly when I was staying with him in Manaus as a kid. I admit that made it easier to contemplate the kill. Sometimes it felt as if the spirit of my grandfather was encouraging me to do it.

I discovered within days that my step-uncle's two sisters – my step-aunts – were not closely involved in the business and actually wanted to sell it immediately but their brother refused.

So, as a first step, I dug up everything about my step-uncle's life at that time. I needed to find a weak spot – a place or an event that would give me an opportunity to engineer his death. And I admit that I got some twisted satisfaction from watching him going about his day-to-day business, knowing that he would soon pay the ultimate price.

Finding an opportune moment turned out to be remarkably easy, as he was living alone in my grandfather's old ranch and used to drive himself to all the company's logging sites in the rainforest.

One day I stopped him on an isolated road. He thought I was a robber. I wore a bandana and spoke with a Portuguese accent. He didn't have a clue it was me, which made the job even easier to carry out.

I took him at gun point to an area of the forest that was being flattened by loggers. I'd been there the previous evening to set up my plan, which included earmarking a half-cut-down tree as the perfect spot. Once we reached that same tree, I tied him to the base of the leaning tree and warned him he would be shot if he moved an inch.

Just before I ensured that that tree fell over with him tied to it, I let my bandana slip down the front of my face. It was a reckless move, but I wanted him to know who I was in the moments before he died. But I don't think he recognized me even then. I'd been a piece of nothing to him when he'd greedily pushed me out of my grandfather's house after he died. My face meant fuck all to him then and it meant nothing now. But just knowing my face was the last thing he'd ever see made me feel even more satisfied that I was about to bring his miserable life to an end.

I let the tree fall over and crush him underneath it. Then I stepped forward, cut the ropes and took them with me. The tree had crushed his head with such force that it ended up at a grotesque, twisted angle with his death mask looking up at me. There was definitely fear frozen in his eyes.

My step-uncle's body was found a few hours later by some loggers he employed on slave wages. Those indigenous people believed he got what he deserved, as he was far more brutal with them than my grandfather had ever been. They were convinced an evil spirit had killed my step-uncle in that "accident", and in a sense they were right. They "celebrated" his death by kicking and stamping on his corpse before the authorities arrived at the scene.

Initially, I worried that those indigenous people might be accused of murdering the man they so hated. But even the local police were happy to see the back of him. He'd long since refused to pay them the bribes my grandfather had so happily given them. I was also told that my step-uncle's sisters and ex-wife and even his kids were extremely relieved he was dead and sold up the company to that same corporation almost immediately after he died.

The success (and perhaps the ease) of that first job definitely fuelled my desire for more commissions from H. I liked the challenge and the feeling of complete and utter satisfaction once a job had been completed. It felt as if I'd found a natural vocation in life, despite all my initial reservations about it all. I'd already started a "real world" job in the fossil trade, which would provide me with brilliant cover for my hitman jobs, so everything was falling into place.

While that first kill was significant in many ways, more importantly, if it hadn't been for that job in Brazil, I wouldn't have fallen in love. My new girlfriend worked for an NGO

(Non-Governmental Organization) helping educate the child slaves often employed by many loggers in the heart of the same rainforest my grandfather and step-uncle had plundered so mercilessly. She was half Thai, half Swedish, so we both knew what it was like to be mixed race in the eyes of others. We both liked the fact that neither of us could be put in boxes. We didn't "belong" to any country or race in the usual sense of the word.

It was her gentle and caring nature, as well as her under-stated beauty, that most attracted me to her. She was the exact opposite of my mother. A calm, measured, patient and extremely loving person. She brought me out of my shell after a lifetime of being an introvert with little to say to anyone else.

She was fifteen years younger than me, but we seemed equal in every other way. Our life experiences – good and bad – matched up to our politics and our outlook on the world. I knew I was following in my father's footsteps by having a girlfriend a lot younger than me, though it really didn't seem to matter. I was 37 years old but emotionally I was at least 10 years younger. I enjoyed a few wonderful days with her on a deserted beach near Sao Paulo after that job in Manaus and found it extremely hard to leave her and set off back to Scotland. There had been moments when I almost forgot who I really was and what I'd been doing in Brazil in the first place.

We promised to stay in touch. It was the first time in my life that I'd had a relationship with a woman that actually felt natural and normal.

* * *

Back in Scotland, nothing much had changed. My father had moved an even younger girlfriend into his crumbling stately home, and I was still banished to the cabin, thank God.

H advised me to cut myself off completely in the cabin following that first job, to give myself time to reflect on what I'd done, so that I was fully mentally prepared when he came back to me with more work. He also told me not to use a regular landline phone or pager as they'd leave a trail of electronic evidence, which could provide people with evidence of what we were doing. I was happy to do this, as I looked on the cabin as my sanctuary. It was at the end of a three-mile track off the main road and at least five miles from the main family house. A place where I could unwind in peace and quiet and be almost entirely self-sufficient.

To my other neighbours – who lived at least 10 miles away – I was an eccentric son of a broke aristocrat who'd been banished to an isolated cabin after a family fallout. I couldn't be further removed from my new vocation.

Then I had what I considered to be a stroke of luck. My 73-year-old father died in bed next to his 28-year-old girlfriend.

My father and I had long since become like strangers to each other. I never saw him in the months before he died, even though he was my closest relative and we lived just a few miles apart. At least I had no reason to miss him when he died. And there certainly was no fortune to inherit, either. What little money there was in my father's estate had to go toward paying off taxes, which meant the main house was to be sold. He had stipulated in his will that the trustees should grant me a lifetime lease on the cabin, which was a pleasant surprise for me as I thought I'd have to vacate it after he died.

But there was another surprise in store in my father's will. He'd asked that I be given a letter he'd written shortly before he died. In it he stated that I wasn't actually his child. I'd been the baby my father was supposed to have adopted in Brazil and brought back to his first wife in Scotland before he went and seduced my indigenous mother.

Instead of being confused, I felt vindicated by the news. It turned out that my mother had got pregnant with me by a man in her own tribe, which made me 100% indigenous. This was a relief, as I didn't want to be Scottish because that would have made me more likely to turn out like my father, whom I hated. It also helped explain the way my father had treated me, especially after my mother went for that swim and never came back.

After reading that letter from my father I became determined to find my real father, so I contacted my girlfriend in

Brazil and asked her to try and track him down for me. In many ways, my life was unravelling like a real-life soap opera, with twists and turns coming thick and fast.

H attended my father's funeral to offer support, as he knew I had no direct family left. I was very touched in one sense, but I also wondered if he was there just to keep an eye on me, particularly since we'd agreed to keep meetings to a minimum to ensure our business venture remained as discreet as possible.

When I saw H that day, I noticed that his injures had deteriorated since I'd last seen him. His lisp had become much more pronounced and he admitted the constant headaches had got so bad that he could only sleep if he consumed enough cannabis and alcohol to knock himself out.

A number of times H sneaked out the back of the house during my father's wake to smoke a joint. I didn't blame him for trying to kill the pain that way. I was starting to realize that, because of those disabilities, in many ways he was living vicariously through me. He'd been a trained assassin before I was even in short trousers, but now that life was completely unattainable to him. No wonder he'd lured me into the killing game.

To be fair to him, though, he was the one with potentially all the best contacts to bring in any work. I was already starting to think I was in this game to counteract his madness. I can assure you, he was 100 per cent crazy. Crazy but brilliant, all at the same time.

If I was a character in a movie, I'd be the one of us two who represented the normal world that an audience can truly relate to, and H would be my mad-scientist friend. Everything about H's life was unbalanced. He was the one who lived and breathed like the devil. He had good reasons for turning out like that, though. Life had been hard on him.

We'd already been through a lot together and knew more about each other than anyone else did. Without H, I would not be telling this story. He was my mentor, my Svengali and the person who turned me into a hitman.

CHAPTER TEN
BAGGAGE

I'd just seen H off from the wake when a taxi arrived outside my father's manor house. It was my girlfriend from Brazil. She'd lost her job with the NGO and decided on a whim to fly out after I'd told her about my father's death and the revelation that I wasn't his child.

Within minutes, she sat me down and held my hand and told me that she'd actually been fired after using company facilities to track down some members of my mother's tribe, and that she had eventually found two of her sisters. My real father had been the tribesman Te whom my grandfather said was my uncle after he shot him.

Te had spent so many patient hours helping me to forage and track animals, and even taught me how to handle explosives. He'd died at the hands of my grandfather after that dreadful accident.

Despite my shock, I wasn't that surprised by what she told me. I'd always had an affinity with Te and was glad to know he had been my real father. What this did, though, was alter my opinion of my grandfather. Not only did I now realize he wasn't even my real grandfather but also that he'd had no right to hide the identity of my real father from me, and certainly no right to end his life, either.

My girlfriend also told me that while she was researching my real family she discovered that my supposed grandfather's greedy adult son – who'd kicked me out of Brazil so he could claim all that inheritance – had just died in "strange circumstances" only a few weeks earlier, at around the same time I first met her. I brushed over that remark, but it was like a reality check – one of the few occasions when my two extremely diverse lives had overlapped.

My girlfriend moved in with me in the cabin that night and never left. She clearly saw herself as being on a rescue mission to save me from my own demons. I wanted to be as open as possible with her, but I had to be extremely careful not to tell her anything about my new "job" with H. I'd already had that close shave with her and I needed to make sure there were no more crossovers.

Equally, she had her own baggage, and we soon started opening up to each other. It made us bond even more quickly and I liked the way she never made me feel bad about anything. It was something I wasn't used to.

I was in a transitional state at that time. I needed a "real" person to guide me through normality and counterbalance the madness of my other life. While I was very happy to have someone to share my life with, though, I knew H wouldn't be pleased, as one of the primary reasons he'd recruited me in the first place was because I was single and living in virtual isolation.

Before I could tell H of her existence, my girlfriend got pregnant and we decided to get married. It all happened very quickly.

The truth is, we moved in together without really knowing each other. We'd fallen in love with love, or with an image of a person who had all the traits and characteristics we thought we craved. And my inbuilt fear was that I might repeat the familiar patterns I'd failed to learn to avoid from my own mother and father.

At that time, there had been a long lull since the first job, and I'd started to wonder if H would ever come up with any more work. And now I was going to be a father, I didn't want to be either absent or dead. I hoped that being a parent would give my life some real meaning for the first time. So I contacted H and told him I'd decided to end our business "arrangement". He immediately asked me why and I finally admitted to having got married without telling him.

H had warned me right from the start that we were only safe if we didn't tell anyone about what we were doing, so he sounded irritated when I told him about my new wife and soon-to-be new arrival. He pointed out it wasn't as easy as just walking away. He said there was a lot at stake. I didn't really know what he meant by that, but I decided not to press him on it. He insisted I went away and thought carefully about my decision. Rather than have a row with him, I agreed, but my mind was already made up.

A few weeks later, my wife lost the baby. She was understandably devastated, but – to be honest about it – there was a side to me that felt a bit relieved. I was still so haunted by the shooting of that boy in Beirut that I'd convinced myself I didn't really deserve to be a parent. I kept thinking that, as I'd deprived his parents of seeing their child grow up, I shouldn't have the right to bring another child into this world. Also, I felt bad about letting H down. After all, he'd saved me from the scrap heap.

A harder side of my personality had gradually emerged following that first job, and that part of me wanted the freedom and excitement that came with a commission to kill. So I contacted H and told him I was still in.

Also, I still had a powerful desire to keep secrets. I knew perfectly well I was doing something behind my wife's back, but keeping that secret from her and the rest of the world seemed to empower me. If I could keep this secret "other life" going, then I felt like I could have it all.

Maybe I simply wasn't equipped to lead a normal existence.

H didn't sound at all surprised when I told him my decision. Not stopping to question why, he announced very casually that he already had another job for me.

To many of you reading this, I must seem to have had such a low opinion of my wife in order to turn my back on her to work for H as a contract killer. But it's not that simple. I'd already gone down the road of being two different people, and neither of them could now exist without the other.

CHAPTER ELEVEN
RISK FACTORS

The military is the perfect place to learn how to detach yourself from the emotions that you should feel when you end someone's life. Many in the armed services try to treat death as a joke, in order to help them handle it. I can see why. It makes it much easier to kill people, if you don't allow the reality of what you've just done to sink in.

There was a constant "connection" between H and I on that level. We understood each other without having to even say much. Despite this closeness, in those early days I had no inkling that H had set up our killing business after encouragement from certain "powerful forces".

* * *

My second job for H was an Iraqi man allegedly selling arms to rogue players in the Middle East. This guy had once been a middleman between Saddam Hussein and the US government, but he'd supposedly turned bad and had been providing arms from Western suppliers to Saddam's sworn enemies, the Iranians. This was the late 1990s. The first Gulf War was long over, but the spectre of Saddam Hussein continued to cast a huge shadow over the Middle East.

It was essential right from the start of our business to have a "shield" between me and H and the actual clients, so that no one could connect us. That's where the "instigator" came in. He was the bridge who gave us that distance. The commissioning process is a finely tuned balancing act. You have to be careful not to press an instigator for too many details in case that leads to problems before, during and after a job.

Anyway, the instigator on this second job furnished H with the background information I needed in order to begin the preliminary stage of the job, the research. My target lived on a typical Middle American housing estate near Los Angeles with his wife and two children. I reiterated to H that I was not prepared to do anything that might put his family in danger, as we'd agreed that collateral damage would never be part of any job.

I began monitoring his movements and discovered that his family were due to be away for a coming weekend. So on that Saturday, I carjacked him after he came out of a car wash, pointed a .22 at his forehead and got him to drive his car straight back to his house, knowing it would be empty of other people.

Once he was in his garage, I tied him up in the driver's seat and got out and attached a pipe to his exhaust. Then I donned a gas mask, started the car engine and waited. He took about 20 minutes to lose consciousness, but I stayed at least half an hour longer to make sure he was gone and carefully wiped away any tell-tale signs before leaving the garage. His body was discovered the next morning by one of his Mexican gardeners.

Naturally, his family were upset and mystified by his death, but I hoped that in the end they'd get over it.

But afterwards, the instigator warned H that Saddam's agents might come looking for us to get revenge in order to convince their enemies in the Middle East that they hadn't played a role in the death of that arms dealer. That warning came via the CIA, who were really saying that if we disclosed anything about the job to anyone, they'd help Saddam's agents track us down and kill us. The number one problem about all jobs is that you can't always pick and choose your clients.

It's the same with guilt. I suppose I had a bit of guilt back then. But I learned to place certain emotions in these separate boxes inside my head. That way, guilt only kicks in when an innocent person is in harm's way. If that happens, I'm as prone to a meltdown as the next man.

Mind over matter: that was the key to my job from day one. You make sure your mind filters out the reality of what you're doing or else you might wake up one morning and put a gun to your own head. At the end of the day, though, and I cannot deny it, *nothing* is the same after you kill another human being. You sleep with one eye open for the rest of your life.

I often hear about hitmen in places like Colombia who rack up four, maybe even five hundred kills during their career. That demeans my profession in many ways. Each and every job should be an art form in itself, as far as I am concerned.

Most of those contract killers in Latin America and elsewhere don't even bother with any pre-planning. They usually kill people off the cuff, which does mean they're not likely to lead long and healthy lives themselves. It's all very well being prepared to kill someone for money, but you have to have an intricate plan to make sure that, if it does succeed, you don't end up dying too.

The real professionals consider all the risks very carefully. They want to survive. You weigh up everything as there will always be room for error. I can assure you that even the best of us make mistakes.

Even with just two jobs under my belt, I'd fast discovered that the head was the most important weapon of all. I learned to remain calm. I tried to not get emotional, as that's when mistakes are made. I knew I needed to park my anger elsewhere, as it would only push me into making a mistake that could cost me my life.

Most build-ups to jobs tend to be nerve-wracking. You need to feel out your intended victim without having had any prior knowledge of them. That's when you can be at your most vulnerable. Sometimes I even run through everything in my head and create a list of reasons *not* to do it.

But some problems are way beyond your control, especially when an instigator and their client are unrealistically impatient to get the job done.

The third job H brought in had the potential to be much more troublesome than the first two. The target was a supposedly much-loved Las Vegas-based billionaire, and the instigator told H his client wanted this man to die in such a way that it looked like an accident but that his closest enemies would still know he'd been murdered.

It was a very specific set of orders, but H warned me that, if we didn't do it that way, not only would we lose a fee of $350,000, but the client would put a hit team on us to prevent us from ever talking about the job.

This billionaire businessman had made his fortune in the clothing retail trade. But on the way up the greasy pole he'd accepted a £250,000 investment from a notoriously hard-nosed criminal-turned-businessman. The investment was eventually paid back in double, at half a million pounds, a couple of years later.

The same company floated for more than a billion dollars on the stock market not long after that, and this criminal-turned-businessman realized that his original investment had been worth many more millions than the money he'd received. The billionaire refused point blank to pay him any more, though. The second time our client went back to ask for some more money, the billionaire promptly threatened him with a writ. Hiring lawyers to tell old-school criminals-turned-businessmen to fuck off isn't always a good idea.

This same criminal discovered from his own friends inside the underworld that this billionaire regularly used contract killers himself. This left the criminal understandably fearing for his own life, convinced that the billionaire would hire a hitman to kill him. So this job really was a matter of kill or be killed. The instigator told H the client clearly needed to get in first before he was topped by his enemy's hitman.

When H first told me the details, I was a bit sceptical, to say the least. The instigator might well have been bullshitting and just using us to finish off a rival. But H didn't seem bothered, and pointed out that the money was so good that it didn't really matter either way. This criminal's instigator even insisted to H that the job wasn't just about the money, either, which H told me in the brief, but which I found hard to believe.

It was simple; this man had crossed a line and he had to die. Why the instigator would try and make it personal was beyond me, but it takes all sorts, I guess.

I spent a couple of weeks in Vegas surveying the target and his life, trying to get a feel for all his habits – good and bad. As I mentioned earlier, I call this the research stage of any job. Looking and listening. Learning and watching.

I usually try to never leave a trace of my presence anywhere I work. For this Vegas job, I'd booked into an anonymous chain hotel close to the airport. Transient travellers between flights went through there on a daily basis, so it was perfect for staying under the radar.

After spending some time on the case, I realized the billionaire was a much nastier piece of work than our client. In public, this guy projected himself as being dedicated to charities and doing good. Yet he was running sweatshops in Bangladesh, where local workers were paid a dollar a day to produce high street clothes lines.

Then came another ticking clock. The instigator came back to H and warned him that my intended victim had indeed commissioned a hit on our client, so I needed to get the job done as quickly as possible. At least the billionaire didn't know he was in my sights. This was important. If he knew, he'd no doubt offer his hitman a big bonus to bring forward the job and to target me as well.

Back in the surreal, surgically clean, tree-lined avenues of Vegas's upper-middle-class suburbs, I established that the only time my man was "vulnerable" was when he went out on his own for an early morning jog. He always ran on a route that took him along the edge of the nearby desert and on to a pathway overshadowed by small, rocky hills covered with massive boulders.

The big day turned out to be a misty morning, which was perfect for what I had in store for him. And of course he didn't have a clue I was about to end his life.

I'd dressed for the occasion, with a construction worker's hard hat and a high-vis jacket, as that sort of outfit would not raise any suspicion if I was spotted by any witnesses.

I watched him leave his house and fired up my rental car and headed for the spot he'd reach after crossing the highway and taking that pathway through the desert. A few minutes later I stepped out from behind a boulder as he came running along and pulled my snub-nose .22 out and waved it at him. I would never have actually used that weapon, but he wasn't to know that.

This is often the moment when intended victims try to bribe their way out of trouble. Indeed, this billionaire did mumble an offer of a million dollars if I'd run off in the opposite direction. But no amount of money he paid me would stop the client from coming after me if I didn't go through with the contract. The temptation simply wasn't worth it.

So we walked about another 50 yards to where I'd already established was the perfect spot. He tried to say something else as we stood there, but his voice was drowned out by the grinding jet engines of a Pan Am Jumbo swooping above us after having taken off from the nearby airport.

Then I pressed the tip of the snub-nose into his kidneys and ordered him to lie face down on the pathway. A few moments later, with him still trembling on the ground, I pushed a boulder that I'd loosened a little earlier down the small hill toward him. And that was that.

His body was found later that morning by another jogger.

The police had no doubt it was a tragic accident. The instigator said his client was delighted with the way he'd been "taken care of", and less than 24 hours later we received the second 50 per cent of our fee. You never get the full amount up front... the movies haven't lied to you.

* * *

The following day, I was back in Scotland driving through the West Highlands past villages, lochs and forests. It was late, so I knew my wife would be asleep by the time I got back.

I finally turned into the long dirt track to the cabin just after midnight. As I got out of my car, a slight drizzle was falling, which left a dusky haze through which I could see the loch next to the forest glistening in the moonlight.

When I got to the outside steps up to the cabin, a light came on in the sitting room. I could just make out a shadow, a human form. I stood perfectly still for a few moments, making sure it was who I thought it would be. The light went out before I reached the front door.

When I finally got into bed my wife stirred and mumbled something. I urged her to go back to sleep.

"How did it go?" she said, under the impression I'd been to Vegas to meet a "fossil client".

"Oh, fine," I replied. "You should go back to sleep."

"That's what you always say."

Then she turned over on her side so her back faced me.

That gave me an opportunity to silently gather my thoughts and try to sleep off the remnants of the adrenaline still running through me after that job.

But now I realize those were moments when, instead of shutting her down, I should have asked her about her day and what was running through her mind. I was already so immersed in my secret life that I was losing the ability to think through anything from someone else's perspective.

CHAPTER TWELVE
TRAPPED

My wife told me once I had an unhealthy and twisted ability to be good and bad almost at exactly the same time. She said it's massively confusing for her. While I do know it's happening, I can't really do anything to stop it.

Her own father had been bad *all* the time when she grew up. So whenever she saw glimpses of that in me it must have caused her a lot of anxiety. But it was only later I realized the significance of all this. I was already so wrapped up in my job with H that I'd created an imaginary line between that evil world and the so-called "normal" world I occupied with my wife.

And naturally I would never once have even contemplated admitting to her, or anyone else for that matter, that getting rid of someone and ensuring no one else even suspected they'd been murdered did feel pretty satisfying. The trouble with most criminals, and a lot of military people, is that they want the world to fear them and have people killed publicly so everyone knows about it. The key to my special skills is the absolute opposite. I had to ensure no one realized my victims died at the hands of a hitman. All jobs needed to be measured and artful. Not brutal and nasty. I had to think everything through very carefully, and part of that was making sure there was a body. That would round everything off very neatly.

It's the planning that separates the men from the boys in this game. I would never just fire a gun. That's the simple, old-fashioned way and it usually ends up getting you in trouble. From Beirut, I knew only too well what happened when guns were fired indiscriminately, and I didn't want to be haunted by any more incidents like that.

H and I believed we'd created a "methodology" for all types of job that was unique – distinct in our own way. But then again, if there were any other versions of me out there, they'd no doubt be keeping their skill sets to themselves as well.

The most important thing is to always remember that whatever method you use, it *has* to work and it *has* to be unrecognizable from another job. It would only take one clever detective to start comparing cases from the accidental death files and I'd be in trouble. That might sound bloody obvious, but many so-called professionals fall apart when they don't stick to these two golden rules.

I've always presumed that the majority of hitmen stay in their own comfort zones and use the same tried and tested skills on each job. That's another reason why I vary my methods and locations so much. Those types of habits can help others to point the finger at you.

* * *

Whenever I was back in Scotland, I was hard at work carefully developing the "normal" version of myself: a gentle, nature-loving person who chilled out at his cabin in the forest with his beautiful wife.

This domestic version of me even had a special "uniform" that consisted of unwashed dark blue Wrangler jeans, a checked shirt, denim jacket and Timberland boots or decks. No tattoos, despite being pressured to have them in the Legion. No jewellery, except a cheap fake Rolex watch.

In Scotland I drove a 10-year-old Jeep Cherokee, which I loved, even though I rarely took it more than 30 miles from the cabin. I even got it converted to LPG to help save the environment. I also used a fold-up bicycle that I often took on the train down south to save on taxis.

I paid for all my travel tickets and other expenses on my fossil business credit card to cover my money trail, just in case anyone tried to investigate us.

While pretending to do so, I had actually become genuinely interested in fossils, which was great and perfectly matched up to the other, environmentally friendly version of "me". I knew it would take some years to build the fossil business up, but it was the perfect camouflage for my work with H. As well as requiring extensive travelling, there was also an eccentricity about it which made it about as far removed from being a cold-blooded hitman as you could get, so I felt comforted that people would never know.

To the outside world, I was a multilingual, fast-emerging business entrepreneur. I spoke English, Portuguese, Spanish and French. I came from a supposedly posh family in Scotland.

The reality was a completely different kettle of fish.

* * *

Throughout this time, I was thinking about H's character much more and trying to decipher who he really was. We'd been in such a whirlwind since Beirut that I hadn't properly considered certain aspects of his personality, despite putting my life on the line for him.

H's backstory was even more chaotic than mine. His life had initially frozen after that truck bombing. He knew only too well that he should have died from those injuries, and he told everyone in the hospital that I'd saved his life, but that's not true. His own determination to live saved him. If anything, I owed him much more for the way he covered me after I shot and killed that young boy on the stairway.

Getting to know his life at that time was difficult because, despite living so near to each other, we both continued avoiding meeting if possible. It was better for security that no one knew we had a connection. H even conceded that coming to my father's funeral had been extremely risky and that he would not be doing anything like that again.

The internet was just starting to emerge at this time, but H insisted we didn't use computers, for the same reasons he had banned the use of landline phones earlier. The only phones I was allowed to use for "work business" were pay-as-you-go burners that I'd usually throw away after a handful of calls.

I felt very reassured by H back then. He was giving me valuable advice and I knew he was doing all this for the safety of both of us. He also urged me to create two or three stash holes in the forest where I should keep the burner phones fully charged and only have one in the house at any one time in case anyone found them. By "anyone" I knew he meant my wife.

* * *

Those three jobs actually turned out to be our only commissions for nearly two years, as 9/11 sparked a shutdown of many major criminal activities. US law enforcement used the terror attacks as an excuse to pursue some of the world's richest criminals, even conveniently claiming that many had links to the money launderers who supplied the funds to the 9/11 hijackers.

The security services in the UK and US, whom H had links to, also didn't want any jobs to be carried out during that sensitive period because of everything going on following those terror attacks. They were obviously hyper-sensitive about anyone finding out about their connections to us.

So I turned to my "day job" as a fossil dealer. I'd been very fortunate to stumble on a career that actually had the potential to be highly profitable in the long term. There were a lot of tycoons – including fast-emerging overnight billionaire Russian oligarchs – looking for huge "statement" fossils (similar to the size of one of those boulders I'd used on that job in Vegas) to put in their huge mansions and vast yachts. Indeed, fossils were becoming must-have items for the world's wealthiest citizens. Ironically, a lot of the clients I began coming across in the fossil world reminded me of some of the type of characters whom I presumed sent instigators in to see H for a new job.

In early 2003, H announced that the post-9/11 problems had fizzled out and that we could now safely reboot the business. But my fossil business had started to take off, so I wasn't even sure I wanted to continue. When I mentioned all this to H, he laughed out loud and told me to snap out of it. I could tell from the edgy tone in his voice that he was far from happy that I would even consider prioritizing my other life over our business venture. Just as he had done previously, H told me to take a couple of weeks to think about it all.

During these weeks, my wife and I had a very nasty row because she still hadn't got over losing our baby and had become obsessed with getting pregnant again. It was the first real argument we'd ever had, and I found it hard to handle. I'd always had a dead side to my character that was built around avoiding confrontations. I never lost my temper, I would just withdraw. But on this occasion my wife demanded a reaction from me. Instead of having a serious debate, I clammed up. I was scared that I might do something really nasty if she pushed me any further. The only answer seemed to me to leave and cool down, so that I didn't screw up our relationship.

I'd already started to feel trapped in that cabin and the other side of me longed for an escape route, which is why I told H I was ready to work again. He even assured me this job would be perfect for my domestic life. It was located in the UK, which meant I wouldn't be away from my wife for long.

CHAPTER THIRTEEN
WATCHING THE DETECTIVES

Fear is probably the single most potent force inside all our heads, and it should never be ignored. I've often wondered if you can be addicted to fear. Most of us don't recognize it in ourselves, but it is there in everyone in some form or another. Youths become street gangsters because of fear. Nations declare war on their enemies because of fear. Kids in playgrounds beat up other children because of fear. You get the picture.

But there is an upside to fear. Fear makes us sharp and alert and determined. This was always great for me, but my next intended victim seemed to have no fear whatsoever. He'd even told all his family and friends he was not scared of dying and knew there was a bullet out there with his name on it. That wasn't going to make him any easier to kill, though. This same man had even told one criminal associate: "Let the fuckers come and get me. I don't fuckin' care. I'll 'ave 'em all. They're the ones shittin' themselves."

We'd been commissioned by a gang boss from south-east England to take out this criminal, who'd shot dead two of that gang boss's brothers in a south London pub following a long-standing territorial feud. H assured me it was a clean and simple job and there would be a big fee. The crime family also came highly "recommended", although their instigator actually proved a hard negotiator when it came to our fee and beat us down to £150,000 in the end.

The instigator for this job insisted the target could only die by accident – not suicide – in order to avoid a gang war that would rip apart the south-east England underworld.

Anyway, it wasn't hard to get a handle on my man's movements. He always drank on his own in the same pub on a Monday night, come rain or shine. One night, I was watching that pub during a thunderstorm, complete with bolts of lightning and buckets of rain, on a mild, mid-spring evening. I'd planned to follow him home from the pub in order to try and work out some good potential locations for the kill between the pub and his flat. Sat outside the pub, I watched a number of customers walk into the premises. They all seemed to be late-middle-aged, typical of the types who still used such taverns on a regular basis.

I was just getting a trifle bored when I noticed a man dressed in dark clothing turn up on a scooter. He stopped and flipped his machine onto its stand. He held himself very upright and kept his helmet on, so it was impossible to tell how old he was.

I could just about tell from the way his silhouette moved along the backlit outside wall next to the pub that he must have been fairly young.

Seconds after he entered the main entrance of the pub, I noticed a youth fiddling with the same scooter before firing it up and driving off on it. This all happened inside two minutes. It was a rough neighbourhood, so I wasn't surprised by the theft.

Then I heard what I thought were a number of loud bolts of thunder crackling in the sky overhead. Just before the third one, I looked into the large front bay window of the pub and noticed a bright flash inside the premises. Those three bolts had been gun shots.

The same dark figure walked confidently out into the driving rain seconds later and disappeared off in the distance, without even bothering to check on his scooter because he already knew it had gone.

I didn't need to go inside the pub to realize I'd just been beaten to the job we'd been commissioned to do. This shooter had gunned down the man I'd been paid to kill and made it as public as possible, which was the exact opposite of how I was supposed to kill him.

I quickly dusted myself down and realized I had to be certain the hit had been successful, so I waited until flashing blue lights, yellow crime-scene tape and a crowd of rubber-neckers started gathering outside the pub. I even heard one old boy standing near me saying: "Fella's been shot. Must be a contract job." Not far wrong there.

Two detectives eventually showed up and I watched them outside the pub entrance literally scratching their heads. Then the double doors to the pub swung open and paramedics pushed a gurney out onto the pavement at high speed. My intended victim looked in bad shape. His arms were flopping down by his side and all the colour had drained out his face.

The crowd gathering behind the crime-scene tape blurred into the blue-and-white flashing lights sweeping the parking area outside the pub. I wondered if the shooter was in the crowd, come back to gloat.

A finger of lightning shot out of the sky and illuminated the gothic wrought-iron gates at the entrance to the park next door to the pub.

I fired up the engine of my rental car and waited. A few moments later, I moved off the curb and followed the ambulance. As I drove, I called H on my throwaway mobile and explained to him what had happened. H was weirdly amused at first and seemed to think I was joking. Then he got serious and agreed with me that the first thing I should do was to make sure the man was actually dead.

I continued behind the ambulance as it slowed down in the late-night traffic. Drinkers were spilling out of pubs just as other, younger clubbers were pouring into the same entrances. When the ambulance turned off the main street into the hospital, I pulled up by the side of the road and got out of my car. Moments later, paramedics gingerly emerged from the back of the vehicle carrying him on a gurney.

I approached, careful to avoid my face being caught by the overhanging CCTV cameras.

"Is he alright?" I asked.

One of them looked me close in the eye.

"He's gone, mate."

The paramedics disappeared through the plastic swing doors into the A&E department, as I retreated back to the warmth of my car.

Despite this reassurance, I still needed to be absolutely certain he was dead. I parked the BMW up nearby on a proper parking space and waited about half an hour. Then I slipped into the side entrance of the hospital and took the stairs down to the morgue in the basement of the hospital. It was nearly midnight, so no one was around as I entered through the double doors. His body was laid out on a slab of marble.

I moved alongside him and glanced down at him for a few moments, just to be certain it was him. I felt a strange mixture of relief and sadness. Relief because the job had reached a satisfactory conclusion without me even having to kill him. Sadness because here was a man in the prime of his life, who'd simply trodden on the wrong toes and paid the ultimate price.

I wished him no ill will, personally. And I really hoped that all the violence committed in his name and those of his mortal gangland enemies would die with him. But somehow I doubted it.

* * *

The instigator for the job told H his clients were furious that the other hitman had beaten us to the job. But H pointed out we should have been warned that another hitman might be on the trail of the man we'd been commissioned to kill.

It turned out another old-school gang had put the hit on him and didn't care who knew about it, and may well have even wanted our clients to get blamed for it as well.

In the south London underworld, many criminals quickly learned it had been a contract killing, which was the opposite of what had been requested. At first the instigator tried to demand we returned the first 50 per cent. It was typical old-school criminal haggling and H said he found the whole process "most distasteful". In the end, the instigator reluctantly let us keep the first 50 per cent, despite suggesting we set it all up deliberately to make it an easier job for us to do.

The inevitable gang war erupted, and I feared those paranoid south London gangsters might still cause us problems in the long run.

CHAPTER FOURTEEN
COVERING TRACKS

Meanwhile H's consumption of drugs and alcohol seemed to escalate in line with the increasingly severe pain he suffered as a result of his injuries. Sometimes it seemed like he was gradually killing himself from the inside out, knowing full well that those injuries would eventually finish him off. Looking back on it, H clearly had mental health issues from the moment he was blown up in Beirut. At the time, I was just worried that his drugs and drink lifestyle might impact on both our futures.

One night, H texted me on a burner phone and insisted I contact him, so I made an excuse to my wife about fossil business and left the house to make the call. He turned out to be drunk and stoned and asked me if I'd help him kill himself. I calmed him down and tried to change the subject, but in the end he hung up.

I went back to the cabin quite shaken by what H had said, to find my wife very irritated about why I'd sneaked out to make a phone call. I did tell her that I'd had to speak to an old friend who was threatening to commit suicide, which I hoped would be enough to convince her that the call had been completely innocent.

My wife was sympathetic at first but when she asked who my friend was, I stupidly clammed up and didn't give her an answer. In my desire to change the subject and in the hopes that it would cheer her up, I said I was going to try and get her pregnant again. It must have sounded a bit clumsy, to say the least, because she looked stunned.

My baby "plan" was dependent on our sex life returning to what it had been like at the start of our marriage. That night we tried to make love, but it didn't work out. As we both lay in bed afterwards, she asked me if I'd ever cheated on her. I said truthfully "no", but I could tell she didn't believe me.

So she tried a different tactic and started extracting childhood secrets out of me with a knowing look on her face as if she was ticking off a list of probable causes for my infidelity. At first, she focused on my relationship with my mother, but when that became too intense I tried to divert everything by turning the conversations back to her. She talked about her father and his treatment of her, but then ducked out of mentioning any more details when it clearly became too uncomfortable for her.

The following night I went to bed early to escape yet another intense grilling, and she went off in a huff for a walk in the forest. In bed, I flopped on my back and looked up at the ceiling for ages thinking about how to handle my marriage problems.

I needed advice and the only person I could turn to was H. So I leaned out of the side of the bed and opened the door to a small bedside cupboard. My hand moved around inside it before I managed to pull out its false wooden back. Behind that was the one pay-as-you-go phone I kept in the house to monitor texts from H.

I noticed there was a message on the phone but I couldn't quite read it and then remembered I needed my reading glasses. It took another minute to locate them from where they'd fallen on the floor next to the bed. I looked out of the bedroom window to make sure my wife wasn't back from her walk and punched out H's number.

Initially, H pretended that we'd never even had that previous phone conversation during which he'd threatened suicide, and got quite angry about me mentioning it. Then he burst into tears and admitted he'd been struggling to "keep it together" since his wife died. I think he was manipulating me in order to get me to open up more about my marriage – and it worked.

I began pouring my problems out to H. After I'd finished, there was a long, measured silence on the other end of the phone line as he thought about how best to respond. He made it clear she was my responsibility, which sounded pretty cold. Then he changed the subject and mentioned a new job.

Instead of being upset by his indifferent attitude to our marriage problems, I was actually quite relieved at the thought of a diversion from my frosty, newly suspicious wife, so I encouraged H to tell me the whole brief. When we'd finished, I put the burner phone behind the false wall to that small cupboard, totally unaware that outside my wife was watching me.

CHAPTER FIFTEEN
THE BIG CHEESE

Being a successful hitman has a lot to do with work ethic. You're only as good as your next job, not your last, so I liked being left alone to make sure I had as much control of it as possible.

The simplest jobs should have been the ones from straight-talking instigators who knew exactly what they wanted and appreciated the volatile state of the marketplace, so to speak. They'd keep well out of the way once H had been briefed, which meant I was left in peace to do what I did best. But there were always unpredictable jobs. They came in all shapes and sizes.

Welcome to Kent, the so-called Garden of England. This is, perhaps surprisingly, one of the most popular places in Britain to carry out a hit. For beyond the rolling fields, golden corn, converted millhouses and luscious green pastures (as they say in the tourist guides) are dozens of deadly old-school British criminals who've graduated from the mean streets of London and bought themselves isolated farmhouses where they can break the law with impunity. They know full well that here the local police are either too overworked or over-bribed to do anything about them.

It was down to one of those very same old-school villains that I was hanging around on a cold and blustery January day somewhere in the middle of Kent. I was watching my next intended victim – a 21-stone middle-aged drug baron – huffing and puffing as he tried to get out of his Saab convertible in a small car park on an industrial estate. He was more used to something a bit flashier than a Saab. In fact, he was known to tour his manor in south London in either a classic Mark 2 Jaguar or a vintage Rolls-Royce which had once belonged to John Lennon. On this afternoon, he struggled to get out of that rusty Saab, and I watched him from the opposite side of the road.

I always have to be careful here not to provide too many salient details, for fear that the police might connect all the dots and come looking for me. But the essence of what I'm saying is 100 per cent accurate. What I can tell you about this particular job is that my target entered a huge, airtight, refrigerated container in the middle of that deserted industrial estate to inspect a drugs haul. While he was in there, I gently closed the doors so he'd think they'd been blown shut accidently by the wind. The trouble was there was no lock to open on the inside of that container. I heard him banging and shouting for help as I walked back over the road to where my car was parked.

He would have frozen to death within a couple of hours. The workers who turned up the following day to that container base had no idea he was even in there. His frozen body was only found after his wife contacted her husband's business partner and said he'd gone missing. The associate went down to the site, found the corpse and removed the drug haul before contacting the police.

The police eventually cordoned off the scene of his death and the surrounding area, so they could search for clues. This surprised me, as I'd presumed they wouldn't bother after what appeared to be an accidental death. I would have thought it was obvious he'd gone into the container and the wind had slammed the door behind him.

It turned out some smart alec young detective had decided to cover his arse when he learned of the notoriety of the victim. But it was all to no avail. A few days later, the local newspaper ran a story on its front page with the police quoted as saying it had been nothing more than "a tragic accident". I liked that phrase.

The police spokesman even told the paper that my victim might have lived if someone had found him and alerted the police a few hours earlier. Also in the paper was his wife quoted as saying: "I'm devastated. I've lost the love of my life", though I'm not sure I believed her since my earlier research work had uncovered evidence she was sleeping with her husband's brother.

The aftermath of this job taught me a big lesson, and that's why I've mentioned it here. I should have questioned H much more closely about the background to this particular man, but I didn't bother and that turned out to be a big mistake. He'd even given evidence in court against one of the UK's most notorious and deadly gang bosses. He'd lied in court and said he'd seen that same gangster at a murder scene, which eventually led to the gangster getting life in prison.

All this meant my man was most likely under police and/or underworld surveillance when I killed him. In my game, that's bad news. And, even worse, there was speculation that the same crime boss had paid to have him killed, which meant he'd been the one to send the instigator to see H in the first place.

Obviously, we couldn't go to this crime boss and ask him if he'd ordered the hit as he'd most likely have us killed on the spot. This old-time gangster had murdered police officers, criminals and even his own family members in the past. And police bosses wanted to nail that same gang boss for all sorts of crimes, including the death of my victim. We'd been caught right in the centre of a veritable shit storm, and we were worried that we might never get out.

In the middle of all this, that very same crime boss issued a public statement through his lawyers insisting he'd had nothing to do with the death in the container. Shortly after that, my victim's two-timing widow gave a press interview during which she said her husband was not a criminal and had simply died in tragic circumstances. She even blamed his death partly on his obesity and other health problems.

The widow also completely absolved the gang boss of any responsibility for the death of her husband. I then discovered that the gang boss had thrown a lot of money at making sure he was not fingered for this man's death.

A few weeks later, I heard that my target had actually taken a £150,000 bribe from the gang boss not to give evidence against him in the first place, but had told the police and judge everything, despite being paid that hush money. He'd double-crossed them all. No wonder he had to die. As they say in the underworld: what goes around comes around.

We were lucky that job didn't end up costing us dearly because of events that were beyond our control. It was a relief and I swore never again to go into a job without knowing a lot more about a target.

But that is easier said than done.

CHAPTER SIXTEEN
NIGHTMARES

Each and every job was an opportunity to learn new things, as it is with any profession. I thrived on what I call the research stuff. I lapped up watching all my intended victims' movements and uncovering salacious details about their lives. The secrets. The vices. The problems.

I'd developed my own "system" after those early jobs, which had to be effective or I'd be in deep trouble. But at home things were getting tricky. I was talking in my sleep about murder and hitmen and dead bodies. My wife didn't tell me any of this immediately. Instead, she artfully stored it up and waited to see what else came out.

Then one evening – while we were sitting in the lounge each reading a book – she asked me if everything was okay. When I asked why, she mentioned the nightmares. I palmed her off by saying I'd had a few problems with a client who'd bought one of my fossils.

Then I made a stupid mistake. I asked her what I'd actually said in my sleep. She said I kept mentioning Las Vegas. Fortunately, she knew I'd been there on "fossil business" at the time of that job. But her questioning made me feel very uncomfortable. It was clear my wife was looking for answers about me as a person, and this troubled me greatly. And I had a recent warning from H ringing in my head. "*If she works out what we're up to, we'll have to take measures to protect ourselves*", he'd said to me once, as if it was as normal as asking for two sugars in your tea.

A few days later my wife announced that she'd decided to train to be a behavioural therapist. I'd financially supported us both up to then, but she said she wanted some independence and control over her own life. It sounded like she might be preparing for a life beyond me.

I did wonder if maybe it would be a good thing for us, though. She clearly needed a diversion from the angst of trying to get pregnant. Our sex life had completely dried up. No doubt all this must have further convinced her I was having an affair.

I think she also wanted to be a therapist so she could try to prise me open and delve into all those secrets I was keeping from her. She knew I was hiding stuff and she wanted to dig it all up, or so I thought. Luckily, she was going to take several years to train up as a therapist, so I hoped I wasn't in any immediate danger.

All this was starting to make me feel like a caged tiger, though. I often found myself pacing up and down on the cabin porch afraid to go in and talk to my wife, in case she nailed me to the floor with her non-stop questioning.

Yet again, I looked to H for some respite and an excuse to get away for a few weeks, take stock of everything and concentrate on my career as a hitman.

H claimed new instigators were circling and he intended on accepting commissions from at least four of them. It was going to be a busy year.

CHAPTER SEVENTEEN
GARDENING LEAVE

Just because I'd knocked off a handful of men and never been caught didn't guarantee I wouldn't fuck up the next one and end up six feet under or watching my toenails grow in prison. This thought was always in the back of my mind.

The 2005 central London terror attacks had just occurred, so H warned me to be even more alert and careful at all times during the next job. Fifty-six innocent people had been slaughtered during the bombings of tube trains and buses.

That meant police and all other UK law enforcement were being doubly vigilant. So my use of disguises became crucial around this time. If I was out and about on a job it was essential to take such measures in case of CCTV and witnesses. I always went out of my way not to look threatening and tried to appear considerably older than I really am. This would help make me more invisible.

* * *

Apparently, gardens kill more people every year than all the hitmen put together across the globe. This should, in theory, make them perfect locations for a job. They're the sort of places where, if someone dies, no one's too surprised.

Whether it's falling off a ladder or being pricked in the arm by a poison thorn or cutting an artery while chopping some wood, death lurks everywhere in most gardens. And it's much harder for the police to find tell-tale evidence out in the open, where the elements can get to it and mess the crime scene up.

The location for my next job was one such garden, a large one in the English Home Counties. The research stage of the job required a lot of waiting, watching and planning while studying the habits of my next victim, whose home backed onto a huge country park to the west of London.

Shadowing a person can be a risky enterprise. If anyone or any camera catches sight of you, that could provide enough evidence for the police to later pull you in, which is why I try to stay at a safe distance.

Initially I established my latest target's movements, before deciding when and how to strike from the country park. I knew I had to be more creative in order to watch him. I was going to be right in his eyeline whenever he was in his garden. So I turned into a park attendant, with a hat and sunglasses, digging away with a shovel near the wall that separated his house from the park. It gave me a perfect excuse to watch him for hours on end, without causing any suspicion.

There were a few occasions when he did actually look directly at me, but that wasn't a worry as long as he didn't know who I really was. Also, there were dog walkers in the park who'd probably notice me, so I made sure they never got near enough to me to be able to actually identify my face.

Eventually, when my man and his family were out celebrating his birthday, I managed to slip over the wall to his house. Once inside, I tampered with an electric utility vehicle he used every day to move stuff around his garden, so that it would electrocute him the moment he switched it on. I knew it was a sure-fire way to kill him because he never allowed anyone else to use the machine. Then I slipped over the garden wall, strode a quarter of a mile up a path through the trees to the nearest main road and rode off on my fold-up bicycle to a train station three miles away.

My target died the next morning when he fired up that vehicle. His family didn't even realize what had happened until his adult son stumbled on his body after calling out that lunch was ready and getting no reply.

It all went very smoothly in the end because my previous job had made me even more careful and alert to all potential problems.

* * *

The great thing about having an alternate "day job" like being a fossil hunter was that not many people actually knew what it really meant. I could use it for all sorts of excuses and no one would question my working practices.

Fossils were becoming such big business that I'd even opened a warehouse to store and display the biggest and most expensive. Some were worth many hundreds of thousands of pounds. I employed two assistants and one of my cousins from my father's side to help run the warehouse.

While both works were going well, life at home wasn't great. My wife had begun her training to be a therapist, which involved attending classes at a college in the local town. To begin with, it seemed to divert her mind away from us and her obsession with becoming pregnant. She was certainly re-energized by it and clearly looked forward to going to college each day. I liked getting her out of the house. It meant there were fewer opportunities for her to uncover my other life.

When she was at home, she jokingly referred to using me as her "guinea pig" when it came to her therapist training. Despite this interest, I wasn't entirely convinced she really wanted to know *everything* about me. It felt as if she thought she had a duty to dig deep, even if she didn't really want to know it all. At least I hoped that was the case.

There started to be a lot of long silences between sentences whenever anything intense was discussed. Even watching TV together could become awkward. It got so bad I avoided programmes about people with secret lives and, naturally, criminals. It felt as if she was comparing me to all the most twisted characters we were watching on the small screen.

A few days later we went for a walk in the forest. It was mid-autumn and cones and leaves made it slippery underfoot. I was bothered when she refused to let me take her hand. We'd just climbed over a huge, rotting trunk of a felled oak tree when she asked me outright what happened when I served in the Legion. That took me by surprise, because we'd hardly ever discussed it up to that point.

I knew I couldn't just brush her question aside. She needed to hear something, otherwise our marriage really was going to start falling apart. The trouble was that H had drummed it into me to keep all aspects of my "other life" secret, and he'd already made it clear he meant in particular from my wife, as well as everyone else.

I noticed her watching me hesitate to respond to her question, so I took a deep breath and started to tell her how I killed that child on the stairway. It was genuinely hard for me. I'd kept it inside for so long. But at least I was able to honestly convey how difficult I was finding it to talk about. My voice was quivering as I went through everything that happened.

We both ended up in tears. I even told her about the cover-up afterwards, but I didn't mention H's specific involvement. It was a hard day, but her attitude toward me changed after that. She became much more sympathetic and I enjoyed that, though I wasn't sure how long it would last. And I still had H's warning about her going round and round in my head.

While it was certainly helping our marriage for her to want to speak to me more, my wife's curiosity was feeding into my own paranoia. I started to think that she might be secretly recording me, and that led to even more uncomfortable silences between us.

And one day she asked me who I really was. It was one hell of a pointed question. I decided not to answer but felt very bad afterwards. Her question had made me deal very directly with the fact I was hiding so much stuff from her. One side of me wished I could get her to leave me, as that would be safer for her. But when I thought about the consequences – being lonely once again – I realized I didn't really want that to happen. It was a vicious cycle.

* * *

One day, my wife was in town on an errand and I went out to put some stuff in one of the stash holes in the corner of the forest. I'd just started digging one of them out with my hand shovel when I heard something nearby. I turned and scanned around to see if anyone was there but there was no one.

When I got back to the cabin, I found my wife already home and in quite an agitated state, which surprised me since I thought we'd been getting on a bit better. She seemed to want to talk to me about something but she couldn't bring herself to mention what it actually was.

I suggested we both needed safe zones where we'd be able to say whatever we liked. Still in the back of my mind was this whole question of whether she was recording me, so I encouraged us to start swimming together. I'd neglected it since my mother's disappearance. The reminders in the bay were too painful, but I put that aside to try and help our marriage.

As I recall, it was late autumn, as we both wore wetsuits. This did mean we could stay in the water for much longer. On that first day, we'd only got a few yards out into the bay when my wife cut to the chase.

"So? Are you having an affair or not?" she said calmly, as the waves rolled gently beneath us.

I was tempted to confess to one. It would be a lot easier than telling her the truth. But why destroy our marriage when I hadn't actually committed adultery?

Finally I answered her question.

"Don't be daft. Why would you think that?"

She didn't respond but I could tell from the look on her face that she didn't believe me.

We both suddenly seemed to go into avoidance mode, so the rest of our conversation that day in the sea was short and sharp answers to banal questions, before we swam back to shore.

It still felt strange that she didn't pursue the matter, though. I've often wondered why. She probably didn't really want to know the truth.

But, undeniably, from that moment on we started drifting much further apart. Christmas Day that year was strange. We barely celebrated it and both agreed not to bother giving each other presents. On the Boxing Day, she asked me if I had a secret phone. That's when I suspected she must have seen me through the window earlier. But I said "no", even though I knew I sounded lame. At least she couldn't have heard my actual conversation on the phone to H in the bedroom, otherwise she would have asked me more probing questions.

Then H rescued me, albeit unintentionally. When we got back to the cabin, I found a text message on my burner to call him. I made an excuse to my wife and went off for a walk in the forest. H briefed me on a new job and as an afterthought asked me how my wife was. I said she was fine, but I knew he was giving me a subliminal message. H was turning into the ultimate grim reaper, constantly looming over my shoulder.

My wife was understandably upset when I walked back to the cabin and announced I was going away on a job at such a sensitive time in our relationship. It was the day before New Year's Eve. She asked me not to go but I refused.

That was when she blurted it all out. It had clearly been building up for a while. She accused me of having just made a call to my mistress and arranged to meet her to enjoy the New Year in her company. She said my job excuse was bullshit.

I was due to leave the next morning, but that night we slept in separate bedrooms and I had a nightmare that was so vivid and loud that it woke my wife up in the next-door room. I overslept the following morning and found my wife in floods of tears in the kitchen. She demanded that I tell her about my lover.

When I didn't respond, she accused me of "hiding something". She said that during my nightmare I'd shouted out names including someone called H and others. They were the names of the men I'd been paid to kill.

"Who were they?" she kept asking over and over again.

I took a deep breath and told her a pack of lies about working as a government spy. I said that was why I was not allowed to discuss any of it, even with her. She didn't say a word as I explained all this. She was looking right into my eyes throughout the time I was speaking, and she didn't look convinced.

I should have felt awful about abandoning her at such a bad time but for some reason I didn't. So that New Year's Eve I left for my job and she thought I was off to celebrate with my mistress.

It turned out to be a relatively small commission compared to the previous ones, but it couldn't have come at a better time from my point of view. H said he'd got the job through an old forces contact. But he was careful not to tell me much background information, so I couldn't be certain he was telling the truth. I didn't really care who it came from. I just needed to escape the cabin and try to stop thinking about my wife for a few days. It was doing my head in. I didn't know what to do.

It was madness to even think I could do my job properly in the middle of a domestic crisis. Having succeeded with relative ease on most of the jobs I'd done so far, I started to take my eye off the ball. I'd got too cocksure for my own good. No doubt about it.

And that was when things got a bit sticky.

CHAPTER EIGHTEEN
KEEPING A DISTANCE

This job should have been fairly straightforward. But I was battling other emotional issues, which made me ill-prepared to deal with what I was about to do.

My intended victim was a professional criminal who'd murdered an underworld rival. On a poorly lit, deserted south London street, I ambushed him and forced him at gunpoint into the boot of his own car, where I tied his wrists and ankles together and shoved a sock in his mouth. Then I got in his car and headed for the countryside.

An hour later we arrived in a deserted car park which was quite well lit, except for the spot I'd earlier chosen, which was overshadowed by an old barn. This conveniently covered the vehicle in complete darkness. I could just make out the edge of a field behind me in my rear-view mirror.

Once parked up, I killed the engine, turned off the lights, got out and walked to the boot and opened it. He looked up at me from the boot and his eyes froze right on me. He didn't even blink but just stared straight at me. It was unnerving, especially as I was in a jumpy mood, thanks to all my problems at home.

For a few moments, I also froze, and we stared at each other for what seemed like ages but was probably no more than half a minute. I was sure he knew exactly why I was there. He'd no doubt been dreading this day ever since he killed his rival. I was starting to feel sorry for him.

Then I snapped out of it and remembered how H had taught me that it's essential you dominate a prisoner and feel no sympathy before you finish them off. So I waved my gun at him menacingly and pulled him out of the boot and dragged him round to the driver's seat.

I took a bottle of methadone pills out of my jacket pocket and removed the cap with my latex-covered hand. Then I pulled down his gag.

He looked strangely relieved at that moment. I had a feeling he thought I'd changed my mind. I prodded his mouth with the tip of my barrel and told him to keep it open. I carefully tipped the contents of that plastic pill bottle into his mouth before pouring some water in to wash them down. He presumed I'd shoot him if he didn't swallow the pills, so he gulped them down. I pulled the gag back up over his mouth and waited. The strangest thing was that he didn't struggle at all. I kept thinking he'd try something but he didn't.

I didn't have to wait long for the pills to kick in. I managed to make sure that when he did fall unconscious, he slumped to the side of the steering wheel to avoid setting off the horn.

It was so quick, in fact, that I thought he was faking it at first. I undid all the ropes and removed the gag when his breathing started to get really uneven.

The police would no doubt think he was just another male suicide victim aged between 20 and 40. So many men take their lives these days, according to newspaper and magazine articles the world over.

As I walked away, I scanned around the car park for one last check and glanced back at the car to make sure he was still slumped in the driver's seat. He looked like some old drunk sleeping it off after a night on the lash.

I felt a sense of relief as I snapped the air bubbles out of the fingertips of my latex gloves to make sure I could get them off easily. Then I hopped a fence and entered a field. I waited until I was three or four hundred metres away before switching on my torch. I was moving swiftly and with purpose by that time. The silence of that dry evening was only broken by the crunching sound of my black trainers trampling through the frosty grass. I felt so good that I didn't feel the need to look back again.

But after a few hundred yards more, I heard something behind me in the darkness. I stopped in my tracks next to a tree and stayed completely still. I had a feeling someone was out there, but I couldn't be sure. I waited for more than five minutes in complete silence in the darkness but never heard any more strange noises. I put it down to paranoia and continued on.

Getting the job itself done is only the half of it when you're in my game. A perfect hit means fuck all if you screw up the departure and the aftermath. That's why I spend a long time covering all exits.

* * *

Once the car park was far in the distance and I reached the other side of the fields, I located my fold-up bike and rode to a station two miles away. An early-morning train took me back to London where I caught a fast connection to Scotland and, less than 12 hours later, I was driving through the forest that had already provided the backdrop for so many pivotal moments of my life. It felt good to be back home safely, another job completed. Now I could devote some time to saving my marriage.

I was fortunate in so many ways. My mind hadn't been properly on that job thanks to all the shit that was going on at home, yet I'd managed to get through it. I knew I'd been wrong to leave my wife at home alone in the middle of a marriage crisis. But I felt re-energized by that job and hoped I could put that enthusiasm to good use. It was the start of a new year, which hopefully would mark a new beginning for our relationship.

The drive from the station to the cabin took twice as long as usual because of the snow that had fallen while I was away.

But contemplating that my wife would be suspicious when I arrived home late was much more difficult to handle.

It was gone 2 a.m. by the time I finally parked up outside the cabin. I walked nervously in through the front door to find my secret burner pay-as-you-go mobile – usually hidden in my bedside cabinet – laid out neatly on the kitchen table.

It was open on a text message which said: "Does she know?"

It was signed H. My wife had gone.

* * *

I was devastated. I had no idea where she was. I kicked myself for accepting the opportunity to leave the house on that job, but I'd genuinely believed that time away might help me to work out how to save my marriage.

I should have seen the wood through the trees long before this, though. My job as a hitman was the other party in our marriage and it had infected our relationship with a break-down in trust.

It was only after she'd left that I realized that my disappointment and anger had little to do with her and everything to do with my own unfinished emotional business and unresolved grief, much of it fuelled by my job as a hitman.

I'd had my chance to walk away from H and I'd chosen to stay. And now I had, I thought that perhaps he was right, and my wife was not as important as making sure our business venture stayed secret.

H had known for ages that there were problems. He'd confronted me about her a couple of times. But I couldn't understand why he'd sent me that text which my wife read, unless he hoped she'd find it.

* * *

Sometimes the key to my job is keeping my distance. That means from clients, targets, my wife and even dear old H. If anyone gets too close, everything can turn to shit, as I'd just discovered.

I'd let my wife get too close and now I was paying the ultimate price. When she upped and left, I began going through everything we'd ever discussed over and over in my mind, just in case I'd said too much, but I really didn't think I had.

I was tempted to call H and tell him what had happened, but I knew I couldn't. H's only priority would be whether my wife actually knew anything about our business venture.

A few days later, H sent me a text saying he'd pulled out of a potential new job citing "security risks". He didn't give me any more information than that, but I sensed it had a connection to what was happening with my wife. I hadn't told him she'd gone, but I was starting to think he knew anyway.

* * *

On all jobs, my first priority is to come up with a fail-safe plan that would make it appear my victim had died in an accident or committed suicide. Without that, I'm not in business.

That means a lot of professionalism, patience and skill. But most of all, it means originality. It's what enables you to surprise your target but also what helps you get away with murder. If you kill someone in a way that's very similar to another hit, there is a real risk someone will put two and two together.

I had a friend in Hollywood who once said the only movies that became blockbusters were the ones that did stuff you couldn't predict. That would get the audience on the edge of their seats. I was trying to achieve similar results with my own work. By making my methods different from anyone else's, I reckoned I had more chance of escaping anyone who might be looking for me.

That night in the cabin I slept really well, which was strange considering my wife had just left me. I think it might have had something to do with the fact she wasn't there listening to me talking in my sleep during yet another nightmare. Just knowing that no one would hear any more about my secret life was reassuring. I still didn't really know how much my subconscious had already given away.

CHAPTER NINETEEN
CLIMATE CHANGE

A few hours later, I woke up when my throwaway mobile started buzzing. It could only have been one person.

"We have some work, my boy," slurred H. "And guess where?"

It had to be Brazil again. H was always on the lookout for work in Brazil, even though I'd told him not to bother because I had such mixed feelings about the country from my complicated family connections.

H actually insisted the main reason he pitched for so much work in Brazil was due to the fact that it was one of the best countries in the world for escaping the police. I think he may have had a point. It was – and still is – riddled with corruption and life out there is cheap. Most murders remain unsolved, as the police are undermanned and rarely have the inclination to re-examine any accidental deaths. Corruption in Brazil runs right from the president all the way down to the poverty-stricken streets of the favelas.

At that time, the supposedly environmentally friendly green energy business was one of the most corrupt industries of all. Brazil was trying to become a global leader in harnessing wind power. Other nations applauded when the Brazilian government announced generous grants for any companies prepared to invest in erecting the vast wind turbines that now dominate the horizon of so many countries across the world. Those vast machines were still in their infancy in Brazil. Ludicrously over-generous grants were being offered by the Brazilian government to anyone prepared to build one quickly.

But in order to get one of these multi-million dollar grants, a bribe had to be paid to the relevant officials in the government, as well as to the state government, local officials and even the local police. At the top of the corruption tree was one specific high-powered official. This guy was allegedly signing off on 20 million dollars' worth of wind power grants every month and personally making millions of dollars along the way.

One of the biggest wind farm companies in Brazil at this time was owned and run by a British expat, who'd known H since they were at public school together. This Brit told H that the same official had demanded an additional payment of a million dollars, despite already having taken an earlier bribe to sign off on the wind power grant. The British guy who owned the wind farm company had raised the funds to cover this official's original bribery demand but he feared there would be even more payments to make if the official decided to bleed him dry. It was a classic Catch-22. If the British wind farm guy exposed the official his company would most likely go bust.

The Brit had even been approached by henchmen for that same crooked official demanding that the new bribe be paid.

The job was to kill the official. H tried to sell me the mission on the basis that we'd be doing something good for the environment and the country of my mother and father's birth. I ignored him and asked how much money was on the table. It was a good fee, of almost £250,000, even if it was nothing compared to the millions that would have been paid to that crooked official.

I needed to use my fossil hunting as cover and it worked perfectly, as I engineered a genuine commission from an oligarch client to track down and export a rare fossil from a mountainous area in the north of Brazil. My oligarch client even lent me his private jet to fly me back and forth from the UK, so my name wouldn't be on any flight charters.

The job had a tight deadline because my target had told the British wind farm king he'd turn down his grant application if the second bribe he'd demanded wasn't paid within a month.

He lived alone in a vast penthouse apartment in one of Sao Paulo's most exclusive residential districts. He was rumoured to have a Picasso on the wall of his living room as well as at least three sexual partners, including a transsexual beauty queen. He was clearly worried about how many people were out to get him, so had bodyguards with him most of the time, even when he visited some of Sao Paulo's seediest nightclubs. I wasn't keen on setting foot inside a nightclub and ending up on a CCTV screen, and, in any case, my indigenous looks meant that most of the racist club doormen in the city wouldn't even allow me into their premises.

I was getting concerned, but then I had a stroke of luck. My man had a penchant for takeaway Japanese food, which he ordered to be delivered to his apartment every other night. I intercepted a delivery and ensured that the tuna he was going to eat was injected with four times the amount of mercury safe for human consumption. He had a seizure and died a few hours later.

I was finishing off a small bottle of sake in a cosy little Japanese restaurant in Sao Paulo the following lunchtime when I looked up at the TV above the bar and saw his photo on the screen. The report ended with footage of a coffin being put in the back of a black van. That was enough for me.

I didn't eat any tuna that day, but I did hop on a plane to Manaus, where I visited the grave of my real father Te. He'd been buried in a site next to a winding river, close to where the trees in the forest hadn't yet been felled by the illegal loggers who had overrun the area.

I didn't bother to visit my so-called grandfather's nearby grave. I still felt a burning resentment about what he'd done. But a lot of my anger still went toward myself. I had this overriding feeling that I'd caused it all. My wife had admonished me before she'd walked out on me. She'd said I should stop blaming myself for everything, but I couldn't help it.

No wonder she'd had enough.

* * *

Not long afterwards, I read that the same British wind farm king had sold out his company to a massive US corporation for more than a billion and a half dollars. I was tempted to call H and see if we could demand a bonus, but that would have been reckless.

Do not return to the scene of your crime ever. Never talk to anyone connected to that last job again. Make sure there isn't one piece of evidence connected to you, either. If not, you could leave yourself open to big problems.

In my strange world it was never a good idea to count your chickens.

CHAPTER TWENTY
ULTIMATE RAINY DAY

After that job in Brazil, I went back home to Scotland. I kept thinking through all the fucked-up stuff that had happened in my life and wondering if it really was all to blame for my wife leaving.

It started to dawn on me that maybe she had been right to go after all. Honesty, or my lack of it, was at the heart of why she'd left. And at least she would be safer not being involved with me anymore. I knew only too well what H was capable of and if I felt he was keeping something from me, I'd be just as outraged as she was about me.

But honesty wasn't always the right policy. Take that supposedly paedo priest whom my grandfather had killed. Maybe he had no intention of touching me that day he showed me those photos of naked men. Perhaps my own fucked-up paranoid mind had projected his intentions into my head, when they were simply not true. In a sense, I had unintentionally told my grandfather a lie, because that priest hadn't done anything other than put his hand on my knee. I did presume he was about to abuse me because of my own screwed-up past.

I was questioning everything that had happened in my life and doing that while being on my own again was certainly not good for my mental health. I'd always believed I was a loner who could disappear off the face of the earth without anyone knowing or caring.

But that wasn't true. I now needed people as much as anyone else.

* * *

Work continued to flood in after that post-9/11 lockdown. Despite whatever was going unsaid in our relationship, I greatly respected H's honesty on jobs and unusual working practices. He'd frequently drunkenly announce he was already half dead from his injuries "so why the fuck should I care what anyone thinks?"

But when I next talked to H he sounded a lot more sober than usual.

"This could be a tricky one," he said, opening a file in front of him on the desk in the back of his rundown cottage.

He was right.

* * *

I read somewhere that hitmen only ever killed their victims on Tuesdays, because it's the one day in the week when people stick to their routines more than on any other day. That's complete bullshit. If your head is in the right place and you're properly prepared for a job, you can kill any time you want.

And there are definitely some people in this world who deserve to die at any time, in any place. They're the ones who are unlikely to live to old age because they're irritating, loathsome human beings who constantly piss people off. That might sound a bit over-the-top, but I promise you it's true. Now and again, these types of characters pop up in positions of power, wealth and influence.

My next target had been treading on so many toes in Spain that the list of people who wanted him dead was as long as… well, I'm sure you get my drift. After launching the preliminary research phase of the job and finding out even more about my man, I was truly amazed he was even still alive. This guy had had it coming for years.

He originally came from the notorious criminal badlands of Galicia, in north-west Spain, where generations of fisher-men-turned-drug-smugglers had made their fortunes over the past 50 years. My intended victim's father was an accountant for a mega-rich family of old-school cocaine transporters. One day, said target was fortunate enough to bump into a daughter from that mega-rich family in a Madrid nightclub. Within six months, he'd got her pregnant, married her and set himself up as an "art dealer" thanks to a generous cash investment from his immensely wealthy father-in-law. The art world of Madrid was soon flocking to him to exhibit their works, even though he knew fuck all about paintings.

Behind his back, everyone was saying this wide boy was a buffoon, though he didn't seem to care because he was flush with cash and lapping up life in the rich lane. He even borrowed money on the back of his father-in-law's name by secretly remortgaging his wife's £5 million house overlooking the Atlantic Ocean, back in Galicia. He was spotted cruising around Madrid in one of ten supercars he'd purchased, also on the back of his father-in-law's fortune.

His wife was so wrapped up in childcare and Gucci baby slings that she didn't seem to notice what he was up to. Or maybe she just didn't want to know. My man's sharp-eyed father-in-law knew exactly what was happening, but he'd deliberately stepped back and done absolutely nothing about it because he didn't want to upset daddy's girl. And predictably – in the middle of all this – my target had his nose so deep inside a bag of cocaine that he couldn't really see the wood for the powder.

Then the inevitable happened. His heiress wife chucked him out after he got busted by police during a raid on a Madrid brothel, which just happened to be owned by his wife's own crime family. Shortly after this, he was declared bankrupt in the high court, and that's when the father-in-law from heaven turned into the father-in-law from hell. He insisted his daughter cut all ties with the idiot she'd married.

That was when the now bankrupt playboy revealed some dirty snaps of his father-in-law, which he was going to use as leverage. He naturally presumed those photos would be his ticket to survival, but his father-in-law had other ideas. An instigator was appointed, and the murder of his son-in-law was commissioned.

H said they were a heavy-duty crime family and therefore I should be careful, but I was always more cautious than him anyway. After all, I was the one on the "front line" doing the actual dirty work. He just sat back with a big fat joint in one hand and a whiskey in the other while I went on the road.

I soon established my next victim's mundane routine life, as well as his healthy and not so healthy habits. There were loads of creditors closing in on him. Some were high street banks, while others were the type who come and collect their money in person if you don't pick up the phone.

The father-in-law knew that if those debts weren't settled, the heavier lenders would come after him, whereas with his daughter's husband dead he could walk away from the responsibility for those debts. In order for that to happen, the world had to believe my target had passed away in a tragic accident.

I discovered that the police were studying allegations from one of his former business partners that he was at the centre of a massive money laundering ring. Members of two Colombian drug cartels were said to be among his biggest customers, but he'd been stealing a lot of that cleaned cash for himself.

I thought about a Russian Suicide, where you take your target to a high place and offer them the choice, to jump or be shot. That would probably be the easiest way for this guy to go, but it was out of the question as it would have upset daddy's girl too much.

Meanwhile my man's consumption of cocaine was doubling every week. He was on 10 grams of cocaine a day. I considered tampering with his supply but discovered that he was so paranoid about the quality of his marching powder that he paid a friend to be his taster for him. If the coke was substandard it was thrown in the bin.

So I had to go back to basics. He was flashy, reckless and stupid. One of those elements would provide the perfect opportunity to kill him. I was sure of it.

I discovered that this guy had managed to hide a small plane from his creditors. It was kept at a tiny airfield near the northern Spanish city of Gijon. I heard on the grapevine that he had learned to fly years earlier when he worked briefly as a pilot for a drug smuggling ring.

He'd kept the plane for the ultimate rainy day, but he also flew solo every Saturday morning when he was in northern Spain. He'd take his plane out over the Bay of Biscay and spend ages dive bombing and looping over and over in the skies above the Atlantic Ocean, no doubt working off all his tension in the process.

That was my opportunity. I knew from my days in the Legion that there was a way you could rig a small plane's ventilation system to stop providing oxygen in the cabin, so that it would end up pumping out pure carbon monoxide.

My man was knocked out just as he was looping through the clouds near Gijon. Witnesses later said it appeared he'd lost control of the plane and it had crashed nose-first into the sea.

His body was washed up on shore. The mother of his child was allowed to grieve in peace and the father-in-law from hell achieved his dream without anyone being the wiser.

CHAPTER TWENTY-ONE
BETWEEN THE LINES

In order for H to keep pulling in the commissions, he needed a wide and varied roster of clients. Those anonymous donors – as H often called them – couldn't give a fuck whether we lived or died, just so long as we didn't lead anyone back to their front doors.

But a few disturbing holes were starting to appear in our operation. Not only had my wife put a spanner in the works, but H's role in all this was starting to look a lot more sinister than I had thought at the beginning.

There was clearly stuff about our business partnership that he wasn't telling me. Some of the jobs had an "official stamp" to them, which meant our clients were from both sides of the law. I also started to fear H might be capable of pulling a blackmail card out of his pocket if he was determined to get me to do a job I didn't want to do. He certainly had enough shit on me to twist my arm to do just about anything he wanted by this stage.

In this game, you obviously have to be extra diligent at all times, and you've got to somehow stay focused despite whatever other shit is going on in your life. My wife walking out all those months earlier had completely knocked me for six. I wanted to find her and persuade her to come back home, but I still didn't know where she'd gone, and there was this nagging doubt in my mind that if I did find her then it might put her life at risk. She had a sister in London and all the rest of her family were in Brazil. None of them returned my calls. They'd been irritated with both of us ever since we'd married in secret.

I'd continually tried to keep my wife safe by not telling H about her questioning me, in case he really did decide that we had to silence her permanently. The longer she was missing, the more I feared she had worked out everything about my "other world" from my nightmares. She'd also found that burner phone with H's text on it, but it gave me some comfort that she hadn't taken it with her, otherwise I would have been obliged to tell H everything that had happened.

But it was still possible she'd been in to see the police. They could have put her in witness protection, which would mean the next time I saw her would be in court.

The only person I could confide in about all this was H, and he was off-limits because he'd insist on "taking care" of my wife if he thought she knew anything.

I convinced myself I was trying to find her but really I was just going through the motions, because I was afraid of what I'd discover if I did track her down. I decided I needed a bit of a diversion, so I called H and nagged him for some work. He sounded more reticent than usual, which worried me. He asked after my wife and I quickly moved the conversation back to work and he admitted a job had just come in, but I didn't like the tone of his voice.

* * *

They say in the underworld that old-school criminals never die. They just go to hell and come back to haunt you. But before they meet their makers, these criminals tend to get extremely bitter and twisted, which can lead to all sorts of problems.

The type of criminals I'm talking about are the ones that made their names robbing banks and organizing drug deals with the likes of Pablo Escobar more than a quarter of a century ago. My latest target was part of this crowd.

He had recently arrived in Bangkok, Thailand, after a long spell as a guest of Her Majesty's Prison Service in the UK, and originally came from a regional British city notorious for its own self-contained underworld where criminals dominated everything from protection rackets to drugs to prostitution. Before he went to prison, if you breathed in that particular city, this crime king would have heard about it.

In the late 1990s, my man had ended up in prison for a very long stretch, despite the efforts of his many crooked police friends to help him out. But while there, he didn't let prison get in the way of his crime empire. It was rumoured that he made more money while being locked up than when he'd been king of his underworld.

When word got out that he had been released back onto the streets, the crime bosses who'd succeeded him and risen to the top in his absence became understandably worried that he might be planning a comeback.

H said in his brief that some of his gangster rivals wanted to stop him trying to take over the cocaine trade in Thailand, where he was busy assembling a small army of men. At the time, Thailand was fast taking over as the destination of choice for old-school British professional criminals, who found it easier to operate outside well-policed Europe. Many of the Thai coastal resorts attracted more tourists than southern Spain and it was a semi-lawless environment ideal for a certain type of hood looking for warmer climes.

The instigator on this job wanted a cast-iron guarantee that this gangster's death would seem accidental. That way, the underworld would simply accept his demise and move on with their activities without any reprisals, and a war could be avoided.

My man had two adult sons who were undoubtedly cut from very much the same cloth. They'd helped boost their father's fortunes while he was in prison by running all his criminal enterprises for him, and recently, they and their mother had also moved to Thailand.

I'm sure my intended victim knew there was a bullet out there with his name on it, but he seemed to believe he could take down his enemies before anyone got to him.

Within days of arriving to do my research work in Bangkok, I witnessed a meeting he had in a city hotel with two middle-aged policemen from his home territory back in the UK. It became very heated between them, and at one stage he tried to punch one of the cops in the face before being dragged off him by the other officer.

I was so concerned that I contacted H and demanded more details about who the original client was. We had a "house rule" not to take jobs that involved the police.

H went back to the instigator and returned a day later with some "extra details" for the job. Those same two police officers I'd seen at the meeting in the hotel in Bangkok had at one time been on his payroll. They had cleaned their acts up after my target went to prison and had since been promoted to high-powered police jobs in the force back in the UK.

In fact, these same two cops had actually given secret evidence against him all those years earlier in exchange for immunity from prosecution. They'd had their slates wiped clean as part of the deal, and that's how they'd got to the top of the force.

Unfortunately, it was already too late to drop the job. This was even spelt out to us in chilling terms by the instigator and, in any case, we'd already squirreled away the

50 per cent up-front down payment. So I carried on with the commission, despite the fact there were so many troubling issues connected to it.

However, my target had few weak spots to exploit. He'd always prided himself on his clean lifestyle. This guy didn't drink, smoke or take drugs. Money was his only addiction. He didn't even have a mistress to visit away from that penthouse. He and his wife had been together since he was a street dealer in his teens in the early 1980s.

All these types of details are an essential part of the research stage of any job because they often provide you with the opportunities you need to kill someone. The more secrets people keep, the more moments they will be alone.

So I focused on my man's two sons in Bangkok. I hadn't taken much notice of them up to now but decided to monitor them for a few days. Within 24 hours, I observed both boys – in their late twenties – meeting the same two crooked cops who'd had the row with my intended victim in Bangkok a few days earlier. But this time my target was nowhere to be seen. I wondered why.

It was possible those two senior cops had commissioned the job, although I doubted they'd have that kind of money. Sure, they'd both been on the take when my Mister Big was running things back in the day, but all that cash would have long since gone on wine, women and kitchen extensions.

Then I watched a meeting between the father and his two sons at a building site on the edge of Bangkok. Something was said between them and one of the sons had to be held back by the other from hitting his own father. I began to ask if it was possible that his own sons were financing his killing. No wonder they wanted my services, as his boys didn't want anyone – especially their own mother – to know he'd been killed by a hitman.

And, despite all this, I still had to decide how he was going to die. It had to be airtight, as there was clearly no room for error.

My target and his family spent their weekends on a vast estate in the Thai countryside, which he'd put in his wife's name to avoid confiscation. His third son – clearly not a criminal – had developed the property's one hundred plus acres into a working farm. He'd even leased extra surrounding fields to grow corn and graze cattle and goats. It looked like a serious legitimate business, but I heard that my man had been irritated about the farm when he got out of prison and was planning to shut it down, despite pleas from his wife and sons. This seemed to be what had caused the rift between them, so perhaps all three sons had clubbed together to get rid of their father once and for all.

Back in Bangkok, my target was charging around town with two Chechnyan bodyguards, as someone had told him that a hitman was out to kill him in Thailand. That didn't necessarily mean there had been a leak about me, but it was an insight into the connections he had. The odds of me ending his life were shortening by the hour.

To avoid being shadowed, he never drove the same route more than once in succession. He binned his burner phones every other day. He didn't even use a computer. I was on the trail of a man who in many ways was a reflection of myself. But I held on. He *had* to have one weakness, one little chink in his armour.

I went through everything I'd discovered about him in my mind and ended up focusing on a jet ski he owned, which he liked to take out early every morning like clockwork from a beach near his apartment. I watched him from an overlooking cliff and timed him from the moment he got on his jet ski to when he returned to shore. I worked out I had a window of about 15 minutes when he would be far enough out to not be clearly seen by anyone on dry land.

I acquired some ammonium nitrate from a farming equipment company 50 miles outside Bangkok. They sold it as fertilizer, but it was ludicrously easy to purchase, despite the fact it's a highly explosive substance.

I knew all that training in explosives I'd got from my father Te when I was a kid in Manaus would come in handy one day.

I rigged up my target's jet ski the night before with a tiny charge of ammonium nitrate. It was just enough to "cash in" on the vessel's notorious vulnerability for exploding. He was blown to smithereens minutes after going out to sea the following morning.

No one even suggested that his jet ski had ever been tampered with. The Thai authorities immediately announced that it was a tragic accident caused by the fact that some jet skis – including this model – lacked a blower assembly specifically designed to vent built-up fumes. Even the smallest spark would cause this machine to blow up. So many similar "accidents" are reported about this in newspapers or on the TV. We'll never know the truth about any of them, but a large number could have actually been hits.

We were lucky with that job in Thailand. It could have brought us down if those crooked policemen had worked out what was happening. I'd worked hard and I'd worked carefully. I'd tried to cover all exits to ensure I got away with murder, as I did with every job, but you can never be 100 per cent sure you're safe, and there we came close. As the old cliché goes, you make your own luck in this world.

The trouble was that the longer I worked with H the more I started to wonder if he was firing on all cylinders. It felt like he didn't want to walk away from missions, whatever the pitfalls. This job just confirmed that further. The instigator on the Thailand job had either been too far removed from his client or just plain dishonest about the reasons behind the hit. Plus, jobs involving personal vendettas are often the ones that the police usually solve. If H knew the details, he had disregarded that, although we seemed to have got away with it.

H and I banked the second 50 per cent and – despite all my problems at home – I was feeling reasonably happy about my life. And ironically, most of that was down to H. Yes, he was my only true friend in the world, but I still had to deal with the fact that he also wouldn't hesitate to have my own wife killed if he thought she was going to inform on us.

It was a complex relationship, to say the least.

CHAPTER TWENTY-TWO
HAUNTED

After that job in Thailand, I couldn't wait for some downtime in Scotland and reached the cabin at almost midnight, just 48 hours after leaving Bangkok. Heavy rain had cleared the air and everything was tinted in a bluey-grey light thanks to the full moon.

I lit a fire and put my feet up. The buzz from the job was still too strong for me to sleep and I had a ravenous appetite, having not eaten on the plane back. I cooked some pasta and absorbed the heat from the open fire as it spread warmth throughout the ground floor of the cabin.

As with all jobs, I wondered if there would be any comeback from this one. It could be a set-up. I didn't know for sure if H really was on top of things. Someone might even have noticed me tampering with that jet ski.

That evening was a standard period of high mental intensity for me as I waited for the dreaded knock on the door. When that period passed, I might be able to put the job behind me and get some sleep.

At one stage during the evening I went out onto the terrace and stood looking up at the moon and across at the water of the loch glistening in the distance. The two snow-capped mountain peaks looming off to my right seemed nearer than usual because of the bright moonlight, so I decided it was a good time to take a stroll through the forest. Soon I was surrounded by so many trees I could barely see the overhanging moon up in the sky.

After walking for a while, I crouched down and pulled a small hand shovel out of the back pocket of my jeans and started digging just below the trunk of a vast pine tree. Eventually I reached a large plastic container, which in turn held a metal box, a couple of feet below the surface. I took out a key and unlocked the box to reveal tens of thousands of pounds in neatly stacked notes wrapped in see-through plastic film. I took out my three latest burner phones, which I'd bought after my wife had found that one in the house.

As I was double checking them, I thought I heard the sound of movement in the distance. A night owl tweeted eerily from a nearby tree and I didn't look into the darkness again.

When I got back to the cabin half an hour later, I was much more relaxed and had burnt some energy on the walk. In the sitting room, I stoked the open fire, poured whiskey into a glass and knocked it back in one huge gulp. It settled my rumbling stomach and made me feel warmer. I rarely drink, so it went straight to my head, but that's exactly what I wanted.

That's when I looked down at my black trainers and realized I was still wearing the same pair I'd had on during that job in Thailand. I'd completely forgotten to dispose of them. Irritated, I pulled out a small hacksaw from my toolbox and sliced the shoes into many pieces. I took each piece in my hand and cut them all again in half, just to be on the safe side. After that I threw every little piece into the open fire.

I know that disposing of those trainers like that might seem like a fuck of a lot of trouble to go to, but it's the small details that, if overlooked, can come back and haunt you at a later date. I've heard of contract killers who don't even bother to chuck their clothes away after a job. They're probably the same ones who go out and celebrate hits by eating in fancy restaurants and drunkenly end up telling all their mates what they've done.

Those trainer remnants would eventually end up on the compost heap that my wife and I had made earlier in the back of the garden. The thought reminded me of her and made me realize how much I still missed her. It was so frustrating because she'd only left because she was convinced I was cheating on her.

Although her departure seemed pointless, maybe it served some purpose. It was a relief, as long as she was somewhere safe.

* * *

Finally, as the sun began peeping above the horizon, I got up to go to bed. But when I opened the door to the bedroom, I immediately sensed someone was there. Then I smelt a very familiar perfume. My wife was lying there fast asleep. I couldn't believe my eyes. I was happy but shocked that I hadn't even realized she'd been back in the house all along.

I lent down and kissed her gently on the cheek so as not to wake her and suddenly noticed how cold she felt. The door to the en suite bathroom then swung open and H walked into the bedroom drying his hands with a towel. He was grinning from ear to ear.

That's when I woke up, completely bathed in sweat. It may have been a dream but it made me worry even more about my wife's safety. I knocked back another large whiskey to try and make the image of my wife's dead face go away, but it took at least another hour before I finally drifted back to a deep but disturbed sleep.

CHAPTER TWENTY-THREE
TRUST FUND BABIES

Most people believe being a hitman is a young man's job. Nothing could be further from the truth. Most professionals are over 50 and so good at what they do that you wouldn't even realize they'd been somewhere even after they'd gone.

H once admitted to me that many of his tips to me about how to kill had come from mistakes he himself made when he was younger, when he was a hitman for the British armed services. These days they call what he did "black ops", but back in the 1970s it was the sort of stuff no government wanted to admit took place.

It was only after that that H had transformed from being classic officer material in the army into a wild, unscrupulous soldier in the Legion before morphing into "a potted out cripple with a short life expectancy", as he liked to describe himself when he'd had a drink or two and a puff on a joint.

In fairness to H, he worked hard to pull in jobs by nurturing contacts across the entire spectrum, from the Royal family to drug barons. He could talk to anyone. This enabled him to sniff out commissions from all walks of life. Even the richest and most privileged of families sometimes needed the help of a professional, despite living in a different world from the rest of us.

Even with his extensive experience, H was surprised by our next job, though. It centred around a married couple based in Geneva, Switzerland, who were members of one of the wealthiest industrial families in Europe. They both had a heroin habit that many in their rich inner circle knew all about and had turned a blind eye to. And for some years, it had seemed that this pair of trust fund wasters were on the verge of dying from an overdose. Yet somehow they were still alive.

Members of the wife's powerful family hated the way that her husband had come in, married her and turned their heir into a junkie. They wanted to force her into a drug rehabilitation centre and clean her up enough for her to take over the family firm. But as long as the husband was around that was impossible.

The instigator who met up with H told him it was imperative the junkie husband died from an overdose because the family not only knew it was the best way to guarantee no one suspected he'd been killed, but also wanted to "shock" the wife into getting off drugs. The instigator even provided H with the 99 per cent pure heroin that would kill the husband. All I had to do was make sure he took it, which is a lot easier said than done. I had always believed the actual job was usually the easy bit, but on this one that was certainly not the case.

It was highly likely that the wife had her suspicions about her family plotting to kill her beloved junkie husband. So she had to believe without question that it had been an accidental overdose that killed him. H assured me that the aftermath of the job would be dealt with entirely by the family themselves. But that could mean they knew my target was going to be killed and who was going to do it.

Dealing with extremely rich people is always tricky because they don't live by the same rules as the rest of us. They don't know the pressures and pains of our world, what we have to do and care about, and it can be difficult to predict them because in their world none of that matters.

When H asked the instigator how much the family knew, he backtracked and assured H that the family actually had no idea the husband was going to be killed and he was sorry for implying the opposite. The instigator claimed the entire commission came from the trustees of the family company, who needed to take drastic steps to stop the company being financially impacted when this junkie heiress became the next head of the firm.

While this was going on, I was struggling to come up with a way to guarantee the husband died and the wife lived, as they took heroin together and were always in each other's company. H did manage to help out here, by getting the instigator to engineer for the heiress to fly out of Geneva alone for a meeting of her family company at their headquarters in Scandinavia. Once he'd done that, I just needed to find a way to get that batch of pure heroin to the husband.

That's when he did me a big favour. I discovered he had a special delivery system for his drugs, which enabled him to never actually have to meet drug dealers. A member of his staff would be sent out to collect his narcotics in the same estate car each time. The drugs were delivered by the dealer, who'd open the tailgate of the car and place them under the carpet in the back and take the money that was there. This meant the driver did not even have to have any direct contact with the criminal. I knew all this because I'd watched it happen each day for the previous week. That meant I also knew exactly where the drugs pick-up took place.

It felt obvious that the husband would order more heroin while his wife was away, so I sat and watched the house until the staff member drove off and then made my way to the same spot where the drugs were always dropped off. Before the staff member arrived in the estate car, I managed to intercept the dealer and convince him that I was there to get the drugs. He was a tad suspicious at first but accepted a payment (that was much larger than usual) from me and handed over the drugs. I delivered my pure heroin to the back of that estate car when the staff driver turned up. He didn't even notice I wasn't the usual dealer.

I heard that, after telling his housekeeper he didn't want to be disturbed under any circumstances, the husband jacked his pure heroin up in the couple's bedroom after. Even his teenage children were told not to enter the bedroom under any circumstances, so it was only the following day, when his wife got back to Geneva, that her husband's body was found.

Apparently, and very weirdly, she didn't alert anyone and left the house with their children and headed to another property they owned on Lake Geneva. It was only three days later that a maid became so concerned by the smell that she called the housekeeper and they entered the bedroom to find the corpse of the husband laid out neatly on the couple's huge double bed. It seems the wife couldn't cope with the reality of her husband's death and had run away to avoid all responsibility for what had happened.

H was positively glowing after this job. He saw it as a brilliant coup to have worked for one of the richest families in the world, and was convinced that it would help bring in even more commissions in the future.

I wasn't so sure.

* * *

A few days after I got back to Scotland, I was shopping in my local town when I noticed a guy who I'd once been to school with.

It was no big surprise, since it was the same town where I'd gone to that comprehensive. But I caught him looking in my direction and that bothered me because it looked like the same boy whose father had blackmailed my father into paying him a bribe to not go to the police about me selling my mother's tranquilizers on the local council estate. Given I beat that boy up, you could say there was a bit of bad blood between us.

Later – as I drove out of the town car park – I saw him again, looking in my direction. He hadn't changed much since he was that skinny, smirking dark-haired kid with a pageboy hairstyle.

Back home in the empty cabin later that evening, I was more consumed with finding my wife than worrying about an irritating kid I used to go to school with. After more than a year on my own, I felt very lonely without her there. I know loneliness is not a disease, but like a disease, it tends not to be a choice people make, either. And those feelings reminded me of when I was a child living in that huge creaking mansion with my neglectful, drunken parents. I even reverted back to the same built-in voice in my head, the voice that had been the only one I trusted when I was a child.

Like so many people who are in the midst of a crisis, I decided the only answer in the short term was to throw myself into work. In this case, it was the fossil business, as I had to await a call from H with a new commission.

* * *

H finally got in touch a month or so later and I admitted to him for the first time that my wife had gone. I'm not really sure why I told him, but I had to tell someone what had happened. But instead of sounding concerned in a fatherly way, he reacted in a very detached manner and made another of those chilling remarks about making sure she did not threaten our security. That convinced me everything was my fault and that I should never have mentioned anything to H. It was safer for my wife if she never came back. I was starting to get the same sort of feeling I had after my mother and baby sister died: that I deserved everything that was coming my way.

H ignored my flat-sounding answers that morning as he went through the details on the latest job. I knew I needed to get out of that cabin before my mood turned even darker.

CHAPTER TWENTY-FOUR
GOOD DAY'S WORK

I'm old fashioned in many ways. I'd stuck rigidly to my no children, no women, no old folk policy when it came to killing. I'd only murdered men who really deserved it.

And H continued to have this uncanny ability to sniff out jobs from all walks of life. His latest one came via an instigator who represented two immensely wealthy business-men. They ran a huge computer company with my intended victim, who'd stolen so many millions from them that they were about to go bust, unless they could get rid of him permanently.

H managed to get the instigator to recommend to his clients that they paid twice the going rate because they wanted it done very urgently and, strictly speaking, we didn't usually take on jobs that involved "civilian" targets like this one. This meant we were in line for a whopping £500,000 payday between us. The instigator didn't complain, because he was on 10 per cent of that. H refused to tell the instigator how the job would be done, despite the high fee. As usual, the less they knew the better. A client's only right was to know that the man would be eliminated in the manner we were renowned for, but not exactly how or when that would be done. That's none of their fucking business.

H briefed me that this target had late-stage cancer and was about to be admitted into hospital. When I raised an eyebrow, he said the instigator and his clients were fearful that the illness might not kill their once-close friend quickly enough, and that was why he had to be eliminated.

The intended victim being in hospital was good news from my perspective, though. This guy lived on a private estate with more security than Fort Knox, so killing him in his own home would have been very tricky. Hospitals are there to save lives – not take them – and that makes them easily accessible for people like me.

* * *

My uniform of choice for this particular job was low-key black trainers, a baggy tracksuit and a baseball cap. Perfect for crowded, urban environments. I'd purchased all these clothes especially for this commission and would dispose of them all immediately afterwards. I've always been careful on jobs to purchase clothes in an assortment of stores, none of which are close to where I live. Also, the jackets always have to have deep pockets.

On the day I'd chosen to do it, my recognizable features were well hidden from the CCTV cameras scanning the car park at the hospital where my man was being treated. I strolled casually through the main entrance and even managed a pleasant smile at a nurse, who kindly directed me toward the ward where I was visiting "a friend".

I patiently waited for the lift alongside a mother, her young child and two elderly women. Once inside the elevator I pressed number three before turning and smiling casually at the other visitors. The lift slowly rose to the third floor. As the doors opened, I slid my hand deep inside my tracksuit jacket pocket to check on the contents. I walked out into the corridor, and looked right and left before noticing a CCTV camera high in the corner of one ceiling. I was careful not to look up at it, because that's always a bit of a giveaway. You never know who might end up analyzing all that footage one day.

It didn't take long to earmark him. He was dressed in a hospital gown leaning casually against a wall with a mobile phone virtually glued to his ear as he talked quietly into the receiver. I moved a bit closer to him but not near enough so that he would notice me properly.

I'd been to the hospital a number of times over the previous few days, so I knew his routine. His addiction to nicotine was the key to this job.

Anyway, on the day in question, I casually walked right past him in the hospital corridor as he continued talking on his phone. Once I'd got another 10 or so yards past him, I turned for one final glance. It was him. No doubt about it.

And it certainly looked as if he hadn't got a clue about what was about to happen to him.

As I continued walking in the opposite direction from him back up the corridor, I pushed my hand deep inside my track-suit jacket pocket again just to be sure. My little .22 snub-nose friend was in there ready and waiting to help me.

I sat down on a bench seat at the other end of the corri-dor next to an old lady and watched and waited. He was still on the phone. I'd spent many weeks planning everything, so waiting a few more minutes was no big deal. Two of the magic ingredients in this game are timing and patience.

He eventually got off the phone and began wandering up the corridor in my direction. His private room was close to where I was sitting but he didn't seem to have noticed me, although you can never be sure. As he approached, I took my own mobile phone out and pretended to make a call. I knew he was examining me as he walked by but instead of entering his room, he continued on down the end of the corridor. Then he opened an emergency exit door and slipped out.

It was time to go to work. I headed to the same exit, care-ful not to move too fast. In the small hallway by the emer-gency exit steps, I stopped and listened and heard his footsteps climbing the stairs above me. I pushed my hand deep in my pocket and gripped onto my gun and took the stairs two steps at a time.

Above me a door opened and slammed shut. When I got to that same door, I opened it slightly and looked through the crack. He was lighting up a cigarette about 10 yards away on the hospital roof with his back toward me. So I opened the door silently and walked up behind him and pushed the gun in his back and told him to turn around slowly. I then pressed the tip of the barrel deep into his forehead and explained that he was either going to jump or I'd shoot him.

I had no intention of using my gun, but he didn't know that. In the underworld, they often call guns "convicts" because they have a habit of coming back to haunt you. The London police even have a unit of divers whose only job is to recover weapons from rivers, canals, oceans, you name it. So you don't want to use something so obviously found and attached to you.

Anyway, back to that hospital roof. It never ceases to amaze me how people *always* choose the jumping option, even though the odds are pretty much the same for either. But on this occasion, my target seemed remarkably calm considering the choice I'd just given him.

He spoke very softly. "Why are you doing this?"

I didn't answer. It's important not to engage with a victim if you can help it.

"You do know why they want me dead?" he said, nodding to himself.

I ignored him and pressed the tip of the gun barrel into the back of his head, so he wouldn't be able to see if I squeezed the trigger. I then looked down to make sure there were no people below us on the pavement. I had always stuck to my mantra of no collateral damage.

"Just jump, for fuck's sake," I said.

And that's when he jumped.

I'd just earned more than £225,000 (50/50 with H plus commission for the instigator). I thought that wasn't bad for a couple of weeks' work. With that done, I headed for the doorway. Two minutes later I emerged into the corridor on the floor above where my target had been due to receive his cancer treatment. I moved swiftly but calmly, because I needed to get out of the building before news of his jump reached the ward.

Downstairs, I departed via an exit on the other side of the hospital to where he'd been. As I walked back toward the main road in front of the building, I noticed crowds gathering on the pavement. I recognized one of his slippers hanging precariously in a small tree near where he must have landed.

I knew his dodgy business background would be looked into following his tragic death. People would say he was in trouble financially and that the pressure finally got to him.

Less than five minutes later, I picked up my bicycle from where I'd left it, unfolded it and headed back to the hotel where I kept all my own clothes. It often made sense to have a place to "turn around" after jobs like this one. In the hotel room, I stripped naked and placed all my clothes in a large black plastic bag.

In many ways, that hospital job seemed like one of the best. No one ever suspected foul play. The guy had topped himself. Pure and simple. I'd pulled off yet another successful job. No hiccups. No witnesses. No problems of any sort. It had been a good day's work.

That afternoon I dropped those clothes in the plastic bag off at a charity shop. You know what they say; charity begins at home.

After that, I headed back to Scotland. I wasn't a full-time criminal, I still had my fossil business to run. I needed to keep busy and avoid thinking about the wreckage of my marriage. But that job turned out to have been too easy for comfort.

CHAPTER TWENTY-FIVE
BAD COPS

A couple of days later, I was twiddling my thumbs in my cabin feeling sorry for myself because my wife had abandoned me when the full impact of the hospital job hit me like an Exocet missile smashing into a Beirut tower-block.

I spotted a small item on the inside pages of a daily newspaper I'd picked up in town that day. The headline read: POLICE OFFICER KILLED. The story said that my victim – who'd "thrown himself" from that hospital roof – was a serving police officer. H had commissioned me to do a job that broke one of our most important rules.

Shit.

H should have known about this. Or he was conned. On the other hand, I wondered if he'd done it deliberately. I wasn't sure what H was up to, and knew we shouldn't be seen together in public, but those airtight rules we'd agreed at the beginning had to be ignored on this occasion. So I headed over to his cottage to demand an explanation and at least try and clear the air.

H turned out to be remarkably calm about everything and said there was nothing we could do about it and that we just needed to keep a low profile and hope there wouldn't be any comebacks. He didn't sound very convinced himself, though.

The following Sunday, a newspaper ran a lengthy investigative piece about how the man in the hospital had been suspected of police corruption and that was why he'd taken his own life. It looked as if the instigator who got in contact with H had been hired by other crooked police officers, who wanted to stop this guy from spilling the beans. We would never have taken the job if we'd known this was the background to it.

Another newspaper then dug up a string of women who were in relationships with my target. One of these mistresses insisted to a redtop that her lover would never have killed himself. One of his colleagues was quoted anonymously in a newspaper stating that his friend was "most likely" murdered. This was getting worse.

A London tabloid then named and pictured one of the police detectives being investigated over corrupt links to notorious criminals connected to the man I killed. It was the instigator, who'd commissioned the job from H in the first place.

Three days after this, the same officer and a colleague were arrested and charged with police corruption. Neither of them admitted anything and within a couple of days the charges against them were dropped because of lack of evidence.

H called me after he'd read the latest story in the papers and accused me of not finding out enough background about the target before I did the job. I pointed out he hadn't asked the right questions when he met the instigator, either. After hours of squabbling, we both agreed to step back from the business until the dust settled. H said if there was an emergency, he'd text me on one of the burners I kept in the forest.

Three weeks later, two policemen – including the instigator who'd commissioned the job from H – were found dead in a burned-out car in a lock-up garage on the edge of a notorious inner-city council estate. It was reported that they'd been caught in the middle of a drug war between two cocaine cartels. The newspapers branded the two dead men as "bent coppers" whose bosses inside the force were most likely also in the pocket of criminals.

The story eventually faded out and it looked as if everything had died down. But I knew that was a warning to us both to reconsider our business partnership before it was too late.

* * *

As I've said, one of the most important assets on a job is timing: to know when it's the right moment to strike. If you pick the wrong time, that's the end of you – permanently. It's the same with deciding when enough is enough, and that moment seemed to be fast approaching.

I'd always considered I was a cut above most of the characters you find in this game. But at the end of the day, it still boiled down to the lowest common denominator, and all the warning signs were there for us to see. Sure, I'd planned each job much more methodically than most hitmen. But ultimately, I was snuffing out people's lives just the same as everyone else, so I didn't have a God-given right to expect never to be caught.

H and I didn't talk again for some months after that hospital job. Then one day he sent me a text asking me to contact him. I expected trouble when I finally got around to phoning him.

H tried to make everything sound very relaxed. He even made some small talk at the beginning of the call. He joked about how he'd met a contact high up in the UK government recently and discovered I had an unofficial nickname in the spy world: "The Ghost". I wasn't amused, because I couldn't understand how anyone was even aware of my existence.

H insisted no one knew *who* I was but admitted there were rumours about a hitman who carried out jobs like the ones we were given. It still bothered me. I said to H, if so many people knew about the so-called "ghost", there was a risk that one day they might try and find me. H didn't answer but changed the subject by announcing he had a new job for me. I don't know why I didn't turn him down on the spot, but instead I listened and eventually let him talk me into it.

That's when it occurred to me that I was – in some strange and chilling way – addicted to killing people for H. It gave my life such purpose. I know it sounds twisted, but I can't deny that I enjoyed it. A lot was down to keeping a secret – that old chestnut – but there was more to it than that. I didn't really want to change anything, despite how it was impacting the world around me – including the lives of others.

CHAPTER TWENTY-SIX
PULLING THE STRINGS

The uncomfortable truth is that contract killers commit their crimes across the globe virtually every day of the week and – in most instances – you don't even know who their victims were. Whatever that truth does, I don't know.

A lot of my success was down to the way I continued to use those different identities on jobs to the point where I had developed many unique and diverse personalities. They could only coexist, though, if they stuck to their main purposes in life. I could change accents on the flip of a coin, from English to Portuguese to Spanish to French. Nobody would ever work out that I was just one person. If you asked someone to pick me out in an identity parade, I don't think anyone would have been able to do it – unless they'd known me for at least half my life.

I'd enjoyed pretending to be other people ever since I was a child. I first learned how to do it in order to be accepted by those kids on that council estate, and in the end it worked. All of this undoubtedly helped me learn to adapt easily to unusual situations.

Then there was my crazy, so-called grandfather. When I'd stayed with him as a kid, he was always checking his rear-view mirror and scanning around restaurants examining the faces of all the customers in case there was anyone there who didn't quite fit in. He could spot the differences between people, so I learned that and employed it. And of course my grandfather pulled off the ultimate personality change by turning himself Jewish to avoid problems after the war. He got away with it for the rest of his life. As part of his Jewish facade, my grandfather was always highly respectful of Israel and how its people had thrived since the horrors of the Holocaust. "Don't ever cross them," he used to say. "They're tougher and stronger than you."

Which is what was ringing through my head when I received my next job.

It centred around a young Israeli scientist who'd developed his own potent legal high synthetic drug, which was a cheap alternative to cocaine. It was a huge seller to drug barons across the globe about 15 years ago. For those not in the know, synthetic drugs were being embraced by the UK's and Europe's party culture. At the time there was no legislation outlawing these substances and therefore they sold like hotcakes.

But this young Israeli scientist turned drug baron then decided to triple the price of his drugs to distributors throughout the US, UK, Europe and Australia. When criminals in those countries complained about this outrageous price hike, this man threatened to get his friends from the Israeli spy agency Mossad to pick off some of them if they didn't agree to pay his higher prices. So these drug lords clubbed together to pay to have the young Israeli taken out by yours truly. They planned to install their own man in place of him, who would honour all the previous price caps for the legal high products.

The instigator put H under immense pressure to get the job done as quickly as possible, because the criminals behind the hit wanted to get their drug businesses back on track. But they all knew that if he was shot and killed by a traditional hitman all hell would break loose and they could well end up being targeted by the Israeli's Mossad friends.

This job entailed getting into north Cyprus – where the Israeli drug baron lived – and, once the job was completed, getting the hell out of there in one piece as quickly as possible.

North Cyprus couldn't have been more different from Israel. It was virtually lawless and filled with gangsters from all over Europe and Russia. It had no extradition treaty with other countries and was run by a Turkish-led puppet government. One old-school criminal I knew once told me that north Cyprus was the easiest place in Europe to hire a hitman. Narcos from all over the world used this crime-ridden territory as the main transit point for narcotics flowing into Eastern Europe, Russia and the Middle East. If I'd been my target, north Cyprus would have been the last place on earth I would have lived, but he'd apparently moved there after the 2006 war in Lebanon following a fallout with a bunch of Israeli gangsters.

After using my fossil hunter persona to get into north Cyprus, I had the freedom to legitimately travel around the entire country. My latest intended victim lived in a large oceanside property on the edge of a pretty seaside village about 20 miles from the city of Kyrenia. He had two ex-Israeli marines as armed guards on duty around the clock. The house was also surrounded by high, electrified fencing. There were two Humvee's parked in his driveway which were rumoured to be bombproof. This guy knew he was a target.

I then received a tip via the instigator that he was going to meet some Russian gangsters at a hotel in Kyrenia that was owned by a once-notorious international gang of heroin smugglers.

After a two-hour meeting, he wandered out of the hotel without an armed guard and headed to the beach for a swim. I was close behind him. His body was found washed up on the beach the following day by a local barman. The corpse had been mangled beyond recognition by the propeller of a boat, which was a bit of luck because all I'd done was drown him.

The local police concluded that he must have died accidently. There was no autopsy, as they don't bother with such things in north Cyprus, unless there is clear evidence of foul play. The only reason they were able to identify him quickly was because of the IDF (Israeli Defence Forces) tag around his neck.

H should have been delighted, but when I rang him the next day to let him know how it had gone he'd just heard from a contact in north Cyprus that the police had got hold of a description of me and were trying to identify who I was. Given there was no suspicion around the murder, I wondered if someone had intentionally dropped a hint to the police.

I managed to hop on a flight to Istanbul less than an hour after that conversation with H. Luckily there was a very short turnaround before I caught a plane to London.

The death of that Israeli scientist didn't even make the local TV news.

H eventually spoke to another contact whom he described as being "very high up" in the UK government. This man said that Mossad had been shadowing the legal-high scientist for two years because he'd helped develop nerve gas for the Israelis but had tried to sell the same formula to the Saudis.

He hadn't been on the run from Israeli gangsters. He'd fled to north Cyprus in order to continue to operate as a criminal and avoid a Mossad hit squad.

It seemed that I'd just done Mossad's job for them and yet they'd deliberately leaked my details to the north Cyprus police. I wasn't sure how they could know who I was anyway. It felt like the Israelis were deliberately trying to point the finger at us to ensure that they were not accused of involvement in my target's death. We'd been set up by the most ruthless spy network in the world.

H promised to talk to his mate at MI6 and see if he could get Mossad to ease off. Once again, we agreed to suspend the company at least until the dust had completely settled following north Cyprus.

H told me he'd already laundered the 50 per cent down payment on the job. We agreed to keep it carefully stashed away somewhere and only use it for emergencies in case it was linked back to this job in any way. We also decided not to chase the instigator for the second 50 per cent.

Then we both sat back and waited.

CHAPTER TWENTY-SEVEN
RADIO SILENCE

I was relieved to turn my back on the business I shared with H, at least for the moment. I needed time to refocus my efforts on trying to find out what had happened to my wife. I refused to accept that my marriage was over, despite the fact she'd been missing for so long. The spare time would also give me an opportunity to further develop the fossil business, which would be useful given that it could well end up being my sole source of income. So I battened down the hatches and become an honest, law-abiding citizen.

I didn't tell H I was still trying to find my wife, in case he tried to "deal" with her himself. It had been so long since she left that I was becoming increasingly convinced that she might already be dead. It was very possible H had taken that decision without even telling me.

I left more messages with all her family in the hope they might get her to contact me, but they all ignored me as usual.

I didn't want anything to happen to her because that would have been down to me. I still felt extremely protective toward her, even though I also knew she represented the biggest threat to my liberty. While I wanted to be there with her, I knew I could only protect her if I ensured she never found out the truth. Yet again, I wondered if she was better off away from me in terms of her own safety. As a result, there were occasions when I'd wake up in the mornings determined to do everything to find her. But within minutes, I'd be enveloped by the realization of what might already have happened to her because of my job. It held me back. I felt as if I was stuck in a strange limbo, wanting on the one hand to be back with her but at the same time being uncomfortable with that because it might endanger her.

A few days later, my wife's Thai mother turned up out of the blue at the cabin. Standing on the doorstep, she demanded to know where my wife was and when I said I didn't know, she told me I was a liar. She barged into the cabin and found a lot of my wife's clothes still in the wardrobe, which further convinced her I had harmed her daughter in some way. I got even more convinced that H must have killed my wife. Her own mother didn't know where she was, which seemed significant.

When I tried to get my mother-in-law to leave, she called the police, and that was when I discovered that the boy I beat up at school was now a police officer. When two officers turned up at the cabin, I recognized him and became worried, but he calmed it all down and seemed genuinely sympathetic to my plight. At least, he didn't appear to think I'd murdered my wife, and he even convinced my wife's mother that my wife must have just walked out. Before he left, we even exchanged a few old school anecdotes, although we were both careful to avoid any reference to that beating I gave him when we were kids. I also noticed he seemed very curious about the cabin and its history.

Whatever the truth behind my wife's disappearance, I knew that I couldn't split entirely from H until I'd got to the bottom of what had happened to her. And there was another problem. If H had had my wife killed and I suddenly quit, that would mean an instant death sentence for myself as well.

After months of radio silence, H contacted me. He sounded as if we'd last spoken a few days earlier. He didn't once mention my wife, which seemed even more worrying. I shouldn't have wanted to know about the job he was offering but, if my suspicions were correct, I knew I had to play him at his own game, so I said I was up for it. In any case, the fossil business wasn't going as well as I'd hoped, and I needed some more cash to invest into it.

CHAPTER TWENTY-EIGHT
THE ODD COUPLE

It was finally dawning on me that H had been my puppet master ever since the day that child died on the stairway in Beirut. I even wondered if he'd specifically done that so he could control me for the rest of my life. Yet despite all this, I still wanted to trust him, for the moment at least. No doubt my desire for a father figure continued to play into all this and kept me working with H for so long, but there were even bigger issues at stake now.

I could tell from H's behaviour that he was trying to soften me up by dangling a new job under my nose. He seemed ridiculously upbeat and it felt greasy and false to me. I didn't even argue when he admitted that the latest commission broke yet another of our golden rules: I was going to have to take out two people at the same time. They were a pair of Russian gangsters, who owned a hotel in Florida. They were very close business partners and if one survived he'd be certain to come after me, so I had to kill both of them, according to H.

Just the word "Russian" should have been a warning sign about this job. They already had a reputation for being more cold-blooded and ruthless than just about any other gangsters.

But H assured me that the instigator of this job was actually American and that the clients were also from the US. So we decided it was worth the risk. In any case, I needed this job to clear my head and improve my bank balance – *and* so I could use some of that money to try to find out what had happened to my wife.

These two turned out to be classic St Petersburg mobsters. They'd "inherited" the hotel in Florida from a local gangster with a gambling debt, who'd run the business as a discreet, modest money-laundering tool. But the two Russians had walked in and turned it into a crime command centre for some of the richest and most powerful oligarchs based in the US and UK.

It was only a matter of time before the hotel was being flagged up by every law enforcement authority in the land, as well as virtually Florida's entire underworld. This pair must have known that running the hotel as such a blatant criminal enterprise was a huge risk because the local gangster former owner knew from the hotel staff exactly what they were up to.

H was typically cagey about who'd specifically authorized the instigator to approach us in the first place, except that they were "locals". It could have been gangsters or even a law enforcement agency. Then, during my preliminary research enquiries, I discovered these two Russians had even fallen out with some of their own oligarch clients after short-changing them while laundering their illicit cash. But – like so many duplicitous criminals – they had their own "insurance policy", which consisted of secret, highly personal files on many of their crooked clients, which they believed would guarantee they'd never be brought down.

My unique job skills were required because if these two died in a traditional gangster-style hit, it would have sparked an underworld war across Florida. Gang bosses no longer wanted wars with anyone, including the police.

So, back to my two Russians in Florida. I popped into their hotel one afternoon and soon worked out why they were on a kill list; it was clear they were both total liabilities. The pair of them spent most of their time lounging by the side of their own pool with five mobile phones on a table next to them and half a dozen attractive ladies in bikinis draped on sun loungers providing the entertainment between calls on their burners. There was also a conveyor belt of margaritas travelling between them and the pool bar. And both men were sniffing an awful lot while using the bathroom on average every 15 minutes. It was bloody obvious what they were on. I was just amazed that so many oligarchs had used their services in the first place.

But none of this made carrying out a double hit any easier. For starters, the pair spent most of their time in the pool area, which was packed with genuine hotel guests all day and all night. Drowning them there was a non-starter because of all those guests. In any case, two grown men don't tend to drown together in a swimming pool. A double mugging downtown might have been more feasible, but the instigator would not allow that in case it sparked a gang war.

Everywhere I looked in the hotel there was a high risk of collateral damage, which broke my biggest golden rule. No innocent person should be at risk when I'm on a job. I continued to remember Beirut.

The two Russians themselves lived in a vast penthouse apartment at the top of the same tower block. They even had their own private elevator, which went up from the top floor of the hotel accommodation to the next storey occupied by just that one flat.

The key to killing these two was to study their daily routines. Where they went. Who they visited. I needed an isolated moment when they could be dealt with. I spent hours in my nearby hotel room trying to work out the best way to do it. It finally came to me like a twisted plotline in a Raymond Chandler novel – except this was real life.

That night, I monitored the two Russians from the vast hotel reception area until just before it was time for them to quit the poolside and go to bed. I joined them in the lift on the second floor as they headed up to the storey below their penthouse apartment. As all three of us got out, I checked no one was around, and just as their personal elevator door opened I pulled out my .22 and joined them.

They looked surprised when I ordered them to take me to their apartment. There I tied them up on chairs at opposite ends of a very long dining room table. Then I made them tell me where they kept their weapons. After that, I gagged them. I have to say here and now that these two never looked scared. They seemed to think I was just going to give them a beating and maybe a bullet in the thigh.

The following morning, both men were found slumped over opposite ends of their vast dining room table. A police forensic team concluded that they'd shot each other dead in what appeared to be a drug and drink session, during which they fired their own weapons at each other.

Two or three weeks after that Florida job had been carried out, H phoned and said he had some good news. The people behind the hit wanted to pay us a bonus. I lost it with H and told him to put the cash up his arse, because I was convinced it had to be a trap. I was still angry that he'd chosen to ignore one of our most important rules by making me kill two victims. Typically, H then did a complete 360-degree turn and told me the following day he'd given the money back to the clients. But I wasn't 100 per cent certain he was telling the truth, and, in any case, the damage may already have been done.

H and I never mentioned the Florida job again, but I always suspected he kept that extra money. But I let my heart rule my head and didn't confront him about it again. There would have been no way for me to truly know, and in the back of my mind was that same old question about whether he had anything to do with my wife's disappearance.

If I didn't track her down soon, I was going to have to confront him. This weird profession is full of headaches lurking around every corner, which is why I constantly watch my back. And I was facing a completely different type of problem, one that, this time, I had no idea how to deal with.

CHAPTER TWENTY-NINE
UNCOMFORTABLE SILENCES

I dreaded the journey back to Scotland after that job in Florida because I couldn't shake off the anxiety I felt about what might have happened to my wife.

The first night back at the cabin felt very strange. As usual after a job, I was still on a heightened sense of alert and found it virtually impossible to sleep. I kept getting up, making a cup of tea and going back to bed to try again. I must have done that at least three times before I finally managed to drop off.

A couple of hours later, I was woken up by the noise of what sounded like a car door shutting near to the cabin. I jumped out of bed, grabbed my .22 from the sideboard and crept out into the hallway. All I could see outside was darkness. Then I noticed the red rear lights of a car as it moved off in the distance.

Moments later, someone tried to open the back door. I aimed my weapon at the door but decided to wait in the hope they might think the house was empty and go away. I heard the same person creeping back round to the front of the cabin. This time they tried a couple of windows, but I couldn't see onto the porch because the curtains were closed. The intruder moved across the front porch and started emptying out some flowerpots maniacally. There was a scratching noise as a key was pushed into the front door lock, but it wouldn't fit. I'd actually changed it a few months earlier and forgotten to put a new key in one of those pots.

I crept forward, pointed my gun at the door and yanked it wide open.

My wife looked down at my gun in horror.

* * *

Once the shock had subsided, we sat down in front of the fire and proceeded to try and unravel our life together after almost two years apart. While I saw her return immediately as an opportunity to salvage my marriage, H's words of warning about how she might have already talked to law enforcement sat uncomfortably in the forefront of my mind.

She said she'd come back to talk everything through. It sounded ominous after all that time. I was so anxious to get her back that I immediately tried to reassure her that I never had an affair and that she hadn't needed to walk out in the first place. But in a sense that was a lie because I *was* in a relationship – with my job and H.

She said she couldn't even consider getting back together unless I admitted what was going on and talked about the burner phone she'd found before she walked out. She also demanded to know who "H" was. Like before she left, I feared that she might be secretly recording me and that the police might be stationed close by and about to pounce. So I told her "H" was that same troubled suicidal friend whom I'd mentioned to her before. But she dismissed that as lies and we started going round and round in circles.

I even asked her where she'd been while she was away, and she refused to tell me. I was so worried about upsetting her that I didn't press her on it.

She insisted we slept in separate beds that night. But at least she was back home, even though I didn't think it would be for long. She'd definitely changed, although that wasn't such a big surprise. What I couldn't fathom was why she'd really come back after so much time away. There was something else behind her decision, but I wasn't sure what it could be.

She kept asking me again and again whether I was ready to talk to her about my affair, so, instead of denying it, I told her I needed time to work out how to tell her the truth, which must have sounded as if I was guilty as charged. I had to somehow convince her that I was giving her my full story, even though I wasn't, if you know what I mean.

I even stupidly blurted out a third-person story about a criminal whose wife knew her husband was a criminal but decided that his "other life" didn't concern her. She looked confused when I finished telling that to her and asked me if I'd had another life and children by someone else all along and if that was why I was so detached about her pregnancy problems. She also kept asking me why I hadn't tried harder to find her.

Partly to give myself some time to think, I tried again to turn it all back on her and asked her if she'd met anyone while she was away, which was an even bigger mistake. She got very angry and accused me of avoidance tactics.

Our conversations were turning into uncomfortable jousting sessions between long periods of silence. And throughout all this, I kept wondering if she was recording me. I hated myself for thinking that way, but it was there in my head all the time.

I suggested a swim with the high tide the following morning. She reacted suspiciously, almost as if she thought I might try and drown her. If only she realized that my refusal to tell her the truth was actually helping to guarantee her safety.

But her sudden return home had also thrown up some other problems. I now had three burner phones in the forest most of the time, and while she'd been away, I'd got in the habit of going into the forest and checking them for messages from H at least once a day. This meant risking even more marriage problems.

* * *

The following morning, I woke up very early and crept past my wife's bedroom to go out to the forest. As I went through the kitchen, I noticed my wife's handbag open on the counter. There was a ripped, official-looking brown envelope just inside it, which I presumed she must have picked up from the post box at the end of our driveway.

I took the letter out and read it. It was from the police and stated that she'd been interviewed by them and that they would need to interview her again in the near future. It was signed by that same local policeman I went to school with, which seemed a bit of a coincidence. I carefully re-folded the letter, put it back in her handbag and continued out for my walk.

I needed time to think all this through. If she'd given them anything concrete, they would have arrested me by now. I had to keep reminding myself that I hadn't actually told her anything incriminating anyway, unless I'd said something during a nightmare.

The key was to find out why the police had talked to her. That wasn't going to be easy, because I wasn't even supposed to know she'd seen them. But at least, for the moment, we were still under one roof.

* * *

Picking up the phone in the forest, I saw a message from H saying he had a new job for me. Although I didn't want to do it, I knew I had to in order to get to the bottom of what was really going on with him. My wife was back and seemed to be safe, but I couldn't ditch H just yet.

When I spoke to H, I decided to get some stuff off my chest before we started talking business. I told him that my wife was my concern only and that he had to stop interfering. I lied and promised I would deal with her if our security was ever at risk. He eventually came round to my way of thinking, but he was more interested in briefing me on a new job than discussing my marriage problems.

This latest commission sounded like a fairly standard gig, if H was to be believed. I had to kill a runaway British cocaine baron, who'd just fled Spain for Panama. He'd at one stage been an informant for America's Drug Enforcement Administration. H implied that the DEA might be behind the commission but said that he couldn't be sure. The target had been trying to force the DEA into providing him with lifelong protection, so he could continue selling drugs and running all his other criminal enterprises. Naturally, the DEA couldn't be seen to officially hunt people down and kill them, so they needed us to do their dirty work for them.

* * *

When I got back to the cabin after speaking to H and told my wife I had to go away on "fossil business", she looked crest-fallen. Not unreasonably, she asked me where. I told her the truth – Panama.

She said she'd been hoping we'd take a break from the cabin and go somewhere a long way from home where we'd both feel we could be more open with each other. She mentioned a marriage retreat in the Panamanian jungle that a friend of hers from college had been to and dropped a big hint about going with me. In the back of my mind, I suspected she wanted to come because she thought I was going to meet my "mistress". So I broke yet another golden rule and agreed to take her on that work trip. Looking back on it, I must have been crazy, but it seemed to be the only answer at the time.

I told her we'd first have to fly into Panama City so I could attend meetings connected to my fossil business, before flying into the jungle to meet a client. The marriage retreat would be our final stop.

CHAPTER THIRTY
CHOPPY CROSSWINDS

My latest intended victim had one hell of a colourful background. He was a university-educated former rock musician, who'd actually played bass guitar on a few hits featuring 1970s band Jethro Tull. He'd first hooked into the cocaine business in Spain during the early days of the Costa del Crime in the late 1970s. Many years later he was arrested only to be inexplicably released without charge. The underworld correctly presumed he was an informant for the feds, and a price was put on his head. That was why he'd hot-footed it to Panama.

He'd last been heard of in Panama City before disappearing into the jungle. I had a few old contacts in the city, so I decided to start there. I quickly established that he was living on a remote island on the Caribbean side of the country. And while all this was happening, my wife was sunbathing by the side of the hotel pool, where we were staying while I went to "fossil meetings".

I was preparing as usual when, suddenly, the entire job got turned on its head.

My wife and I were queuing up to check in for a twin-engined flight to that remote island when a male passenger behind us commented on what a nice place we were all flying to and asked if we'd been there before. He seemed vaguely familiar as my wife engaged him in small talk. The same man ended up sitting right next to us on the plane. I felt uncomfortable talking to him because I still hadn't worked out if I knew him or not. But my wife didn't seem to mind.

Just before we landed, we hit some choppy crosswinds and the aircraft lurched to one side just as the man next to me was pulling his passport out of his trouser pocket. He dropped it on the floor right under my feet. I picked it up for him and immediately noticed the name on it. It was the name of the man I'd been commissioned to kill. And he didn't look anything like the one old grainy photo I'd managed to find of him during my research work.

The grassy airstrip we eventually landed at was the length of two football pitches and the terminal building was the size of a large garden shed. As we picked up our luggage, I noticed my new friend looking about tentatively. A couple of locals seemed to be watching us. I thought I saw him nodding at one of them, but I couldn't be sure. Yet another surge of paranoia hit me. Maybe they were police and this was all a trap.

As we walked down a dirt-track road from the airstrip, my target directed us toward the only hotel, where I'd already booked a room. He told me he'd rented a house on the other side of town and asked us both to meet later for a drink.

I needed to gather my thoughts. As I watched him stroll off toward the town, I noticed one of those same locals from the airstrip earlier. He was walking behind us, although I couldn't be certain he was following us.

As soon as I'd dropped my wife and our luggage in the hotel room, I went into job mode and headed out on a reconnaissance trip, telling her I had to meet a fossil client.

When I arrived at my man's house about 30 minutes later it was bucketing down with rain. He seemed delighted to have some company and insisted I come into his home to shelter from the tropical storm. He was even disappointed my wife wasn't with me.

Once inside the front room of the house, he slung the same bag he'd had on the plane onto a table and unzipped it with a huge smile on his face and urged me to look inside. It was packed with tightly wrapped see-through plastic bags of cocaine.

"I told you I'd been on business in Panama," he said proudly.

I looked down at the cocaine and sighed. Not only was I socializing with my next victim, but he'd now pulled me and my wife into his own criminal activities. I tried to smile back but he could see I was irritated and apologized about showing me the coke.

He told me the local tailing us from the airstrip was his partner in the cocaine deal. The man was providing protection as there were some other criminals on the island who didn't like him selling drugs on their territory. I wondered if that same "shadow" was watching us at that moment.

Sometimes in life you have to ditch all your carefully laid plans and start again – very quickly. I couldn't carry out this job until I knew exactly what was going on. Under normal circumstances, I would have spoken to H and asked his advice, but I decided not to in case he worked out I had my wife with me.

* * *

Back at our hotel that night, my wife and I slept together for the first time in more than two years. It was a disaster, as my mind was on other things and she thought my impotence was down to my "mistress". My main worry at that moment was not the mistress accusation, but that H would find out I'd taken her on that trip.

There was so much stuff spinning round and round inside my head. Something wasn't right about this job, but I couldn't nail down what it was. I couldn't get to sleep, so I went and sat on the balcony of my hotel room while my wife was asleep in bed. I noticed the same local man – who was supposedly protecting my target – walking past the hotel.

The next morning, I woke early and called the target on a burner phone to see if we could meet. But he didn't answer, so I left a note for my wife and headed over to his house. As I was approaching the property, I passed the same local man again. He was going in the opposite direction. We nodded at each other but nothing more.

When I got to the front door it was slightly ajar, so I walked straight in. I looked through every room in the house but there was no sign of him. When I got to the main bedroom, I noticed that the bag which had contained all that cocaine was now empty. There were three untouched lines of cocaine on the bedside table together with a rolled up twenty-dollar bill.

Then I looked out at the swimming pool through the closed French doors of the bedroom. My target's body was floating face down in the water.

I had no doubt that a local drug dealer had just done my dirty work for me, and by all accounts he'd done a good job, because I could see there wasn't a mark on his body. He looked like a drowning victim. This was perfect. This time I would take credit for the kill. I'd learned from that earlier job in London that honesty definitely wasn't the best policy in this game.

We caught the small twin-prop back to Panama City with just minutes to spare that same morning. By mid-afternoon, we'd arrived at the marriage retreat on the outskirts of Panama City. It was more of a guesthouse than a hotel, but the brochure had promised to "*restore your relationship with yourself, your couple and nature during this romantic and transformative holiday. In an exclusive, small group, five-day retreat for couples you'll learn new skills for coming together as a couple in creating your goals, your desires and your life."*

The first two days at the retreat felt more like a prison camp. A lot of our bitterness with each other was aired and I had to stifle the urge to escape the entire place. But gradually it did begin to do what it said on the bottle and we both started to get everything off our chests. We even started to connect with the marriage therapists after that, and definitely both found it quite helpful.

We rounded it all off on the final full day by taking some local mushrooms and reconnecting on an altogether higher spiritual level. I'd been very reluctant to take them at first because I'd never been into drugs (and didn't want any important information to be spilled) but one of the organizers was adamant that they had a therapeutic effect and, having taken the mushrooms, actually I have to agree with them.

That night my wife and I slept together and this time everything worked. She seemed so much happier and hopeful that we could save our marriage and have a child.

It was an extraordinary turnaround considering how long she had been away.

* * *

But the aftermath of that job in Panama proved to be a lot more problematic than I thought it would be.

The instigator was highly suspicious about who had actually carried out the kill. I couldn't see how they could possibly know the truth, but it did unnerve me a bit. H rounded on me and asked outright if I had eliminated the target myself. I swore that I had, but he didn't sound too convinced by my answer. The instigator refused to pay the second 50 per cent. I told H that they were just trying it on to avoid paying what they owed us. But H was more worried that the instigator's client might turn us in if we didn't waive that second 50 per cent.

And there was my wife. I'd broken all the rules by taking her with me on the Panama trip, and I knew that if H found out, he'd carry out his threat to "deal" with her once and for all.

The strange thing is that I felt worse about lying to H than I did about the threat hanging over my wife. It seemed that despite all the recent dramas, I still had a strong urge to kill for money and I enjoyed maintaining all those separate compartments of my personality.

Despite my commitment to the job, I was starting to feel less loyal toward H by this stage. I should have read my own attitude as a warning sign. But I was so obsessed with mending my broken marriage that I'd taken my eye off the ball.

And H just kept on bringing in more work.

CHAPTER THIRTY-ONE
OFF THE SPECTRUM

When you know how much work it is to get away with murder and avoid detection, it's hard to imagine that there was – and still is – another totally different form of hitman out there. He's a bloke in a pub being paid five grand to pop your mother-in-law. He's probably a crackhead waster with a criminal record as long as your arm and would end up being flagged up to the police within hours of a killing.

Here I was at the other end of the spectrum. No one was supposed to know what I'd done apart from the people who'd paid me and H. But despite all the preparation, more and more cracks were starting to appear in our business. Instigators were coming back to us with information they could only be getting from people who knew exactly what I'd done. That explained why H sounded very subdued as he went through all the details of the latest commission. I deliberately didn't ask him what was wrong because I didn't really want to know.

My latest intended victim was a multi-layered criminal, killer and terrorist who was a cut above most of the usual riff-raff we'd encountered. He was involved in multiple conspiracies across the globe, and I've disguised his identity here even more carefully than usual because those connected to this job wouldn't hesitate to hunt me down if they thought I'd ever talked to anyone about it.

I had my suspicions right from the start about who was behind the commission, but I decided not to mention anything to H. There was one bit of good news, though. The instigator stipulated that the man's body needed to disappear, which made my life a lot easier.

This Lebanese-born target had for many years been raising funds for Middle Eastern terror organizations. He'd settled in southern Europe where he set up a hotel chain that was used to launder hundreds of millions of dollars for terrorists and criminal organizations. While running these hotels, he'd got into a turf war with a European crime boss that resulted in the boss dying and this man taking over one of the most profitable drug-smuggling routes on earth. He was soon dealing directly with the Colombians and handling vast shipments of cocaine destined for Europe, the UK and Russia. He continued channelling a percentage of his profits to those Middle Eastern terror cells, some of whom were locked in a proxy war with the Israelis.

Then – about 10 years ago – the traditional drug-smuggling routes through Spain began to collapse due to increased European law enforcement activity. My target decided to set up an air route flying cocaine across the Atlantic to

Africa. This would be transported by truck up through the centre of the continent into North Africa before crossing the Mediterranean into Europe and beyond.

In order to do this, though, a tame, poverty-stricken, corrupt African state was required, so he homed in on the president of one such tinpot African nation and became his "personal adviser". I can't even say which end of the west African coastline this country is on because it would give the whole game away. This "job" also gave my man the added bonus of diplomatic status, which meant he could travel anywhere in the world without facing the usual security checks.

In my research, I discovered that he had at different times been an informant for Mossad, the DEA and British intelligence. He'd been supplying information to them for more than a decade.

Right now, he was hiding in plain sight, despite knowing he was probably on multiple hit lists. He must have presumed that the security services of those three countries he once "served" would keep him alive because he knew so much about them. But if those Middle Eastern terror cells knew he was an informant for their sworn enemies, no doubt they would have joined the long list of people who wanted to kill him.

Anyway, my target's visibility in the world certainly made it easier to track him down. He travelled in the president's private jet between that tiny African country and his cliffside hacienda overlooking the Mediterranean on virtually a weekly basis. He was so confident of his safety that he had just one bodyguard, a seven-foot giant of a man from Mali. And that was despite the fact that, as I discovered, there had been five attempts on his life over the previous decade.

His social life was dull, to say the least. He spent most of his time watching satellite football matches, especially when he was at his villa, so there was no opportunity there. His one weakness, though, was luxury cars. He had a collection of at least a dozen and everyone living near his palatial home knew all about them.

One day, he was out in his Bentley Corniche without his guard when another car pulled up alongside him and the driver admired the gleaming vehicle. A few minutes afterwards he disappeared off the face of the earth.

I can't say any more about what actually happened because someone might work out it was me. But suffice to say, H billed the instigator for the final 50 per cent a few hours later.

Then something very strange happened. As I was checking out of the hotel the following morning, the receptionist mentioned there had been a call for me the previous evening when I'd been out on that job. The man who'd rung hadn't left a message and even told the receptionist not to mention it to me. But she said she felt obliged to do so because I was checking out.

No one knew I was staying at that hotel, not even H. I put it to the back of my mind for the moment because my priority was to leave that Mediterranean resort as quickly as possible.

That call to my hotel unnerved me, especially when it came to H and our joint business venture. But I didn't share any of this with H, even though perhaps I should have done so. As far as he was concerned, the job had gone well and there was no reason to curtail our commissions.

The local police and press initially concluded that my target had been car jacked and the criminals involved had shot him dead and disposed of his body. But when his Corniche was found after two days at the bottom of a cliff, they announced that he must have had a road accident and his body had been swept out to sea. Although this was the official line, rumours emerged that he had staged his own disappearance because he didn't want to be killed by one of his many enemies.

It wasn't until a few weeks later that H admitted Mossad had commissioned the kill after H struck a deal with them in exchange for them not pursuing us over the death of that Israeli scientist. Clearly, even the killing game is open to some old-fashioned wheeler-dealing. H said he'd had no choice because Mossad would have crushed us if we hadn't played ball with them. I felt used, but there was nothing I could do about it. I am a hired hand after all.

CHAPTER THIRTY-TWO
USUAL SUSPECT

Back at the cabin, the marriage retreat seemed to have helped improve my relationship with my wife. We slept together every night and I hoped we could spend some time consolidating our marriage, because there was usually a gap of at least a couple of months between jobs for H.

But just a few days later I picked up a message to call H urgently. Not only did my wife look irritated when I disappeared into the forest to speak to H, but he told me he had a job and completely ignored me when I pointed out that we usually always had a longer gap. It felt as if H was recklessly taking on any commission that came his way. We were literally turning into a conveyor belt of murder.

His consumption of drugs and alcohol was increasing in line with the fast turnaround of all these jobs, which meant he wasn't even analyzing them properly before accepting a commission. I had no doubt it would all end in trouble.

* * *

I've spent a lot of time in southern Spain over the years. It's not called the Costa del Crime for nothing. The place is crawling with villains from all over the world.

By the time I got there, most of the really big bosses in this gangsters' paradise came from Russia and eastern Europe. Many – as with those two in Florida – were as cold as ice and didn't give a toss about collateral damage. As a result, many of the older, more traditional European criminals – who once dominated this area – were no longer around.

But there was one old-school Irish criminal who seemed to have survived it all. You'd expect a character like him to go out in a hail of bullets in a very public execution, so the rest of the underworld could say good riddance and his death would be a warning to others not to push their luck. But the instigator who briefed H on this latest commission insisted he had to "go" in an accident. Not even a suicide would be acceptable, because that would leave too many unanswered questions, especially about who was actually behind the job. And of course, there had to be a body to prove it, otherwise some clever cop or private investigator might start digging around.

I became fascinated by this man because he was like a walking history of criminality. He'd started life as a street thief orphan back in Dublin in the 1950s. By the 1960s, he'd graduated to pimping girls in sleazy bedsit sex dens. He'd also nurtured the city's two main criminal families of the day. They liked his immaculate tailored suits and handmade shirts almost as much as they liked him, it seems.

Drugs then arrived in Ireland and pushed the sex and robbery businesses into the gutter. My man soon became the middleman for a Colombian cartel and eventually helped flood Europe with cocaine in the early 1980s. Following this, he moved to Spain's Costa del Crime and partnered up with ETA terrorists who provided the best and safest drug transport facilities from the Costa del Sol up to the UK, Ireland and most of Europe.

At the time, the Spanish security service the Centro Nacional de Inteligencia – the CNI – had swamped the Costa del Crime with agents in a bid to crack down on ETA's fund-raising drug supply lines, which paid for arms to kill police and soldiers throughout the country, as well as murdering innocent civilians on the streets of many Spanish cities.

Eventually, my man was pulled in for questioning by Spanish agents. But instead of a long term in prison, they proposed that he could continue as a coke baron if he became their eyes and ears on ETA's activities on the Costa del Crime. He agreed.

Within a few weeks, he'd convinced ETA he hadn't helped the CNI at all and instead was feeding them false leads to enable ETA to continue their widespread smuggling operations in Spain without interference. Then he discovered that ETA were planning to blow up a garrison of soldiers south of Madrid. He traded this information with the CNI for his freedom and headed off back to Ireland before the ETA attack commenced.

A crack unit of Spanish undercover troops killed three ETA operatives who'd planted that bomb in the army garrison, just a couple of hours before their explosives were due to go off. Many accused the CNI of killing those ETA terrorists in cold blood after it emerged they weren't armed when they died in a hail of bullets. Others believe the shooting helped kickstart the first tentative steps toward a peace process, which would eventually come about a few years later.

With this part of his life over, my target had returned once again to his beloved Costa del Crime with a new identity and was soon back to his old habits, smuggling huge quantities of cocaine.

When he heard ETA were looking for him, he went to the CNI to try and save his own skin, but the police ended up arresting him for drug smuggling and he received a long prison sentence. Just a few weeks into that sentence, he was taken in a prison van to a dentist near his prison north of Malaga for some "urgent root canal work". When the van pulled up at some traffic lights, he slipped out of an unlocked back door and disappeared back into the underworld. The escape was his reward for helping the CNI.

Two years after this, he turned up back in Spain yet again telling his old underworld cronies he missed the sunshine and the lifestyle on the Costa del Crime, and he'd been there ever since.

That's when H and I came into the picture. The CNI were clearly worried that if this character started opening his mouth, he could seriously jeopardize the peace agreement with ETA. H told me that the instigator on this job was at least five pairs of hands away from the original client. In other words, we couldn't be sure who was actually behind it, even though it felt obvious it was the CNI.

The man I was charged with killing lived alone in a house high up in the hills behind Marbella, right in the heart of the Costa del Crime. A narrow track twisted up to his home, which ran alongside a ravine that dropped 2,000 foot down to the valley below.

One night, he was out at his favourite brothel when I swerved my car right across that same narrow mountain-side track as if I'd just been in an accident, and waited. A few minutes later, he turned the corner and headed straight toward me. He was so drunk he only spotted me at the last moment and slammed his brakes on. Stumbling out of the car, he offered to help me move my vehicle.

I pulled out my .22. He didn't look surprised and smiled at me but said nothing. He knew.

I gave him a choice: either take the bullet or drive the car off the edge of the road and hope to survive the sheer drop. He agreed to the latter option. I didn't blame him.

He and his car went over the edge of the road and down into the ravine. It was so dark I couldn't see the vehicle, but I heard it bouncing off the rocks as it crashed right to the bottom. I eventually got down to where it had landed and gingerly checked inside. He was dead.

The local media reported that he'd had a heart attack as his car rolled down the ravine, which was a complete stroke of luck, as that guaranteed no one would look too closely at the death.

In the real world of contract killers, there isn't always time to be cool or fashionable or even scientific about each job. At the end of the day, you just have to cover every exit in triplicate and hope that a bit of luck kicks in.

CHAPTER THIRTY-THREE
OLD HABITS

By the time I'd returned home after the job, all that good work put in at the marriage retreat seemed to have faded, and my wife once again started trying to force me to talk about my "affair". She'd been annoyed I'd gone off on another job and she had clearly been festering while I was away. She'd even gone back to sleeping in another bed. We'd suddenly gone backwards and everything between us started feeling doomed again.

A few days after that, I picked up a text message on one of the burner phones I kept in the forest to contact H. Initially I thought about ignoring him, but I eventually called him back.

The first two or three minutes of conversation seemed innocent enough, but H never phoned just for a chat. There had to be a reason behind the call, and when he asked how my wife was, all the pieces fell into place. I said she was fine and tried to change the subject.

Then he asked me if I knew a local policeman who I'd gone to school with. I said I'd never heard of him. It was a stupid response. I should have tackled it in a more open and relaxed manner. H didn't mention the policeman again. He also didn't have any jobs that day, either.

I was starting to think he was having us both watched, after he made that comment about the policeman. Either that or my wife had tracked H down somehow and confronted him, which was an option I didn't want to think about.

My wife noticed the edginess in my mood as soon as I arrived back from making that call to H. She probably thought I'd been making a secret call to my "mistress" yet again.

Later that same day she tried to get me to have a swim out in the bay. I came up with an excuse that I had a cold. She knew I was lying but pulled back from pressing me any further.

That night the atmosphere in the cabin darkened. We became very awkward with each other and I got worried she might walk out again, so the following morning I agreed to go for a swim.

Just as we were about to leave, that same policeman I'd once been to school with was getting out of his car in front of the cabin. My wife seemed very nervous when she saw him. He nodded sternly at me as he approached us. Then he looked at my wife and asked her if she'd received his letter. She nodded her head reluctantly.

When I enquired about the letter as if I knew nothing about it, he said it was a follow-up to a car accident report by my wife. But I knew there hadn't been an accident. Her car was exactly as it was before she took off.

The meeting ended just as awkwardly, when I asked him why on earth he'd bothered coming all that way just to discuss a small car accident. He ignored me and walked back to his car.

That afternoon my wife and I finally made it for a swim and – when we were bobbing about in the calm water – I asked her why she hadn't told me about the "car accident" and that letter.

She sighed and turned to me and asked: "Are you a criminal?"

I laughed and said: "Don't be ridiculous."

We swam back to the shore in silence.

That night at dinner in the cabin, there was an elephant in the room that was getting bigger and bigger by the minute. Neither of us, though, seemed prepared to acknowledge it.

When my wife eventually went to bed early, I stayed up pacing around trying to think through what to do. I kept thinking about the way my wife reacted when she saw him arrive at the cabin and how she ignored my questions about that letter.

The only immediate solution was to quit working for H, but I didn't want to do that yet because I needed to know what his involvement was in my personal life. That was business I wasn't ready to leave unfinished.

It felt like I had all the pieces, but was only really starting to put them together.

CHAPTER THIRTY-FOUR
MINK-LINED COFFIN

In a perfect world, I should have been working like a mercenary. Get commissioned to do a job and try to avoid the rights and wrongs and the consequences of my actions as long as everything comes within my remit. But each job felt more difficult because of all the other shit now going on in my life. I had to concentrate doubly hard on every aspect of my work, and I was growing increasingly suspicious about how certain jobs were landing so conveniently in H's lap.

A classic example of this was my next job. I was commissioned to kill an elderly African leader, who'd originally been catapulted into power following a vicious military coup backed up by old-style mercenaries in the mid-1980s. His reign of terror was rumoured to have even included genocide. The instigator told H the job had to be an accident or suicide, otherwise it would spark a bloody civil war and a lot of innocent people would lose their lives.

The target lived in a vast presidential palace full of bodyguards, and I knew that if I was apprehended on the job, I'd most likely be considered an evil foreigner and they'd string me up.

It was obvious this job had come from someone very high up the food chain of world politics or from a major corporation with a vested interest in the natural resources of this particular African nation. Many large companies operating in Africa have special secret budgets to use for bribery and corruption, which arguably makes them almost as culpable as whoever they are bribing. The president and his henchmen had recently tripled their bribery demands to Western companies on everything from mobile phone networks to oil refineries.

I was readying myself to fly out to Africa, and then, the day before, he was overthrown in a bloodless coup.

H and I were delighted because we thought we'd get to keep the first 50 per cent without having to get our hands dirty. But less than a week after the coup, H heard from the instigator, who insisted the job should still go ahead. He claimed there were fears the now ex-president would mount an immediate counter-coup to get back in power.

He and his three wives had fled to his 20-bedroom chateau in the hills behind Nice, on France's Cote d'Azur. The property had been purchased a few years earlier with £25 million of his blood money. He knew he'd have to run one day.

By the time I got to the Cote d'Azur, he'd installed multiple bodyguards alongside him and his large family in that chateau. Surveillance was hard because he rarely left the property, except in a convoy of limousines, so I bided my time and waited for the perfect opportunity. Over the next few days, I researched him until I found a gem of information which would provide me with a perfect opportunity. It came in his medical record.

Three days later the ex-president boarded a train from Nice to Paris with just one bodyguard. There would be an opportunity to kill him on that train, because I knew he had a colostomy bag after an earlier bout of cancer. That meant he visited the toilet very regularly.

An hour after the train journey begun, we were speeding through the French countryside when I watched my intended victim leave his first-class compartment and head to the toilet without his bodyguard. I waited until he'd been inside the toilet for a minute and banged hard on the door. I could hear him struggling to empty the contents of his stomach, so I banged a second time.

He eventually opened the door in a fury. I apologized in perfect French and let him step out of the toilet before pushing the barrel of my .22 into his kidneys. I forced him to the exit door just a few feet away. He looked incensed that I had even dared to pull a gun on him, but he said nothing more. He knew no one would have been able to hear him above the sound of the high-speed express train rattling its way north.

I made him open the exit door himself and held it with my left hand while pushing the barrel so deep into his kidneys that he lost his balance and fell out. He stood no chance of survival at 120 mph.

There were a few raised eyebrows about his death because of his background, but the French authorities were quick to conclude it was either a genuine accident or suicide. A lot of people were very relieved that he'd gone.

* * *

The morning after I got back to the cabin, my wife got notification in the post that she'd passed her therapy final exams with flying colours and immediately announced plans to open a treatment centre in the local town.

At the time, I was torn. I believed that her becoming a fully-fledged therapist could end up being the best and worst thing to happen to our marriage. It gave her a goal and a challenge and could divert her from always asking me awkward questions, but I knew that, as she gained experience as a therapist, she'd start to unpeel the aspects of my life I didn't want to share.

And there was her desperation to have a child, which had gone on for some years. She refused to accept that she didn't seem able to get pregnant. She also remained convinced I had a secret lover, although she didn't call me out on it as much anymore. She didn't need to. I could see the resentment in her eyes.

One day at the cabin, she switched tactics and began once again asking me pointed questions about my childhood. She was digging to work out where my "weirdness" came from.

Initally, I wasn't thrilled about the idea of talking about my past again, but she kept pressing me, so I briefly mentioned the paedophile priest in Brazil and how my grandfather had killed him, even though I wasn't even sure if he was really going to abuse me that day in the rainforest. She looked very shocked, but she composed herself and asked me to talk through it all. I found it hard but tried to be as open as possible and admitted I'd been convinced ever since that I helped kill that priest.

My wife said I was clearly suffering from something called "sensory deprivation". Naturally, I had no idea what that meant back then, but I've since worked out that she's right, because I was, without doubt, deprived of a lot of things during my childhood. I'm still not sure that gives me an excuse for what happened, though.

I hoped that by encouraging my wife to delve inside my childhood she might work out a way to save our marriage – and therefore her life. We seemed to be doing fine and then one morning she asked me if I'd really cared about that baby she'd lost all that time earlier. She said I'd looked so detached when it happened. I could tell from the way she said it that she was not going to give up trying to get pregnant and this was her way of telling me.

A few days after this, H briefed me on a new job and I decided that if I went away for a while, maybe the break would do us both good. I always felt like that was the solution. I should have learned my lesson from before she'd left me that time but I still couldn't let go of the killing game.

CHAPTER THIRTY-FIVE
END OF THE LINE

The next job played a significant role in why I decided it was time to make some big changes.

My intended victim was a criminal who'd killed another gangster. It was a familiar scenario, so I won't bore you with the research details. The job itself took place on a narrow, isolated country lane a few miles north of the busy seaside city of Brighton, in Sussex. I'd stretched a wire across the deserted road at waist height so that my target would run straight into it as he sped down the hill on his Harley-Davidson motorbike on his way to work.

The plan was that he'd lose control of his machine and crash into a nearby wall, which would hopefully kill him on impact if he wasn't already dead. If it didn't, I was on hand to finish him off. After setting all this up, I retreated to a vantage point behind a hedge to watch it all.

Eventually I heard him approaching on his bike. But I couldn't see him because of the high hedges on each side of the lane. He got nearer and finally came into view when he was about three hundred yards away. That was when I saw that his 10-year-old daughter was on the back of that bike with him.

Suddenly, an image of that dead boy in the stairwell flashed in front of my eyes. I scrambled from the hedge to a gate post where I'd attached the wire and cut it with the same wire-cutters I'd used to measure it up in the first place. They sped by on the Harley just as I was ducking back behind the hedge. He and his daughter both looked at me very suspiciously. This was a guy who knew he was a likely target for a hitman. Now he'd caught a glimpse of me, the element of surprise – vital in my line of work – had completely gone out the window.

He must have given his own daughter a ride that morning in order to put off any attempt on his life. Clever or chilling, depending on your way of thinking. The thing that bugged me most, though, was how he could have known what lay in store for him.

* * *

On the train back to Scotland that afternoon, I couldn't get the vision of that child sitting on the back of her father's motorbike out of my head.

I hadn't called H as I usually did. I knew he'd order me to continue with the job, but I wasn't in a fit state to keep going. Everything started crashing in all around me after that. The boy I killed in the Lebanon was still there haunting me, but for so many years I used to be able to shake him off by killing other people. Now, that seemed to be gone. I was in pieces. I couldn't share my issues with H, even though he was the one person I knew in the world who would understand all that stuff.

Eventually, thoughts swirling around my head, I got up from my seat on the train and headed to the toilet at the other end of the carriage. Once inside I was violently sick. I sat on that train toilet for more than 20 minutes shaking and sweating. All the usual feelings of satisfaction after completing a job had been replaced by shame about what I'd almost just done.

I eventually stood up and looked in the toilet mirror for some reassurance. All I saw was a stranger staring back at me. A loud rap on the door eventually snapped me back to reality. It was another traveller wanting to use the toilet.

I tidied myself up, unlocked the door and tried to hold my head high as I apologized for taking so long. But I made a point of not looking in the eye of the middle-aged woman waiting. I could feel her studying me closely, and for a split second I wondered if she'd been following me.

From a professional point of view, the job was a disaster, and personally, there's no doubt it was a definite turning point.

There was still H to consider, though. He'd left a dozen text messages on my phones immediately after that job went tits up, but I just couldn't face talking to him. My life felt as if it had just frozen solid. I didn't want anything to happen to my wife, but I also knew I couldn't afford to be exposed.

My only choice seemed to be to do absolutely nothing. It was a dangerous game plan, because when you stop, it's easier for someone to catch up with you.

ACT THREE

THE MELTDOWN

CHAPTER THIRTY-SIX
THE THINKING FACTORY

So I had walked away from H. It should have felt like a huge weight off my shoulders, but I knew our business together was far from over and he'd be back one day.

After that initial, manic flurry of calls immediately following the Brighton job, he gave me a wide berth. I just didn't hear a word from him. I concluded that he must have decided to avoid me completely, just in case he ended up being caught in some kind of trap. I destroyed all my burner phones in the rather naive hope that that would mean I'd never hear from him again.

I began to focus all my energy on the fossil business, which was attracting some immensely rich clients. One Russian oligarch paid almost half a million pounds for a fossil that had cost me £150,000, and that same client also wanted to put some of his money into helping me expand my business. In some ways, this Russian businessman and his entourage reminded me of the type of people I came across through H's commissions. I made sure to push doubts about him and his men into the back of my mind, so as not to let it affect my business.

The same oligarch eventually ordered an even bigger fossil to put on the main deck of his billion-pound yacht, although this time he wanted it for free in exchange for his investment in my company. I refused his offer, but he took my rejection very personally. It all ended with a nasty confrontation with two of the oligarch's henchmen during which they threatened my life.

Knowing it wouldn't be hard to make it happen, I seriously considered making that oligarch pay the ultimate price, but then calmed down. That evening I even consulted my wife. She was happy that I'd actually involved her in my work, since it was something I'd hardly ever done before. My wife told me to ignore it all and simply stop dealing with the oligarch. She said there was no need to clash with him, which I felt was right.

A few days later, two police detectives – one of whom was that old school friend – turned up at my warehouse. He seemed even more detached and officious than when we'd last met. The two officers said there'd been an accusation that I'd tried to blackmail the oligarch and made threats against him. They also mentioned vague claims of money laundering and tax evasion, but at least there was no mention of my links to H.

They even let slip that the oligarch had hired a corporate intelligence company to snoop on me. The firm had connections to the UK police, whom they'd pressurized to arrest me after a complaint from their client.

None of the claims were true, and I wondered at first if it was a police cover story, so they could investigate me thoroughly, or if maybe those corporate spies had dug something up on me.

I was escorted to the police station and charged – under caution – by my old school friend. I spent more than 48 hours in police custody because I didn't get there until Friday evening and no magistrate was available to consider a bail application until the following Monday morning.

Initially, I was only allowed one phone call, so I contacted the solicitor who knew H and got me out of trouble all those years earlier when I had that fight at my father's regimental dinner. H's lawyer friend promised to travel up over the weekend to help me get bail on the Monday. I was certain he'd tell H I was in police custody, which meant H would be concerned I might be interrogated about our "business". Although, actually, I didn't hear from him.

My wife didn't know I was in prison because she didn't answer the call I was allowed to make to her on my second day in custody. I had thought she would at least wonder where I was, but then I guessed she probably thought I was with my "mistress".

Being in a cell for 22 hours a day gave me a lot of time to think, and I began to wonder if the paranoia was doing some strange things to my head. Had I just been used by H and those spy services as a disposable killing machine all along? Was there any way for me, H and our business to be linked back to our clients? If so, and they found out I was in police custody, they'd surely try and silence me.

I guess you can't have enemies if no one knows who you really are. But I now suspected my former classmate had something against me. I presumed it originated in that fight we had when we were at school together. But what else did he have on me?

And why hadn't H been in contact yet? I started to seriously think that he might have kidnapped my wife since my arrest, or even killed her, to make sure I didn't say anything about our business.

H's lawyer turned up on the Sunday afternoon and organized for me to be given bail first thing the following morning. I asked him if he'd talked to H and he said he hadn't seen him for years, although it sounded like he was lying.

That evening, just before lights-out in my holding cell in the basement of the police station, the same old school friend paid me an unofficial visit. He accused me of working in the drugs business. I laughed. I was relieved because that meant he had no idea about my connection with H. He referred to how he might have to interview my wife as a material witness and made it clear he thought we were living apart. I didn't understand his last remark, and certainly didn't like it, so I refused to speak to him any more and asked him to leave me alone.

Just before he left my cell, he advised me to come clean about "everything" and he'd see if he could put in a good word with the judge at my eventual trial. I thanked him, sarcastically.

CHAPTER THIRTY-SEVEN
DEAD MAN WALKING

The following morning I was released and set off for home.

When I got back to the cabin, my wife was there. I demanded to know why she hadn't picked up the phone to me when I was in custody. She said she'd gone away for a couple of nights and left her mobile at home. Somehow, I had a feeling she knew about me being arrested. When I asked her where she went, she said it was none of my business.

I told her that the policeman I'd been to school with had accused me of being a drug baron, and that it had reminded me of how she'd accused me of being a criminal shortly before I was arrested. I demanded to know if they'd been talking to each other, but she stormed out of the sitting room without answering me. After such a suspicious response, I decided to do some digging off my own back.

My old school mate turned out to be a very strange fish. He lived on his own in a flat in the nearest big town to where the cabin was located. He seemed to work on his own much of the time, which was highly unusual for a police officer, and didn't seem to visit his nearest police headquarters often. I also heard he'd been involved in several sensitive operations in the past, which sounded to me like undercover work.

I picked up rumours on the secret service grapevine that he might be a sleeper agent in Scotland for the UK security services. Even though he clearly had no idea what I was involved with, I was getting worried. I had to keep reminding myself that someone would have paid me a visit or got rid of me by now if they knew about H and I. I began to suspect it could be a test set up by H to keep me on my toes. He was certainly capable of pulling that sort of stunt.

After four or five days of carrying out my own enquiries, I decided that, whatever reservations I had about him, it was time to talk to H. I knew it was risky because – in his own twisted mind – he believed he had the right to kill my wife if he thought she was a threat to our business. So I packed my .22 in my jacket pocket and, against all our rules, headed for H's cottage.

When I got there, H welcomed me in like a long-lost old friend. At first I was suspicious, but when we got inside the cottage he pulled a photo of us together in Beirut out of a drawer and reminisced about the good old days, which did put my mind at ease. We'd been through a lot and he clearly treasured that.

He then made us both a cup of tea, lit up a joint and sat down in his favourite armchair and didn't say another word.

That was always his way of making sure I had to speak. So I took a very deep breath and told him everything, from the truth about that disastrous last job, to my wife on the Panama trip and how I didn't kill the target there, and rounded all this off with an explanation of my own decision to walk away from the killing trade.

After I'd finished, H didn't utter a word. He just nodded at me as if he'd known everything I'd just told him all along. I noticed his face harden in just the same way it had all those years earlier when I'd questioned why he'd covered up that little boy's death in the Lebanon.

Then he coughed and cleared his throat before telling me what he felt were his "two main options". He said the first was to have me killed. The second was to ignore everything I'd just told him and continue working together.

He continued that, before we could do that, we had a problem to sort out because the criminals who'd hired us to kill that man on the motorbike not only wanted their money back but also wanted to find me and kill me in case I talked to anyone. I volunteered to go and see them alone, because all the problems on that job were down to me. H hesitated and said not to worry, he'd take care of it, because he'd "cocked it up". When I asked him what he meant he assured me they didn't know who I was, even though he didn't actually answer my question.

H lit up another joint and sucked in a huge lungful of hash, which drifted out from between his lips as he began speaking again.

"So, how's your missus coping with all this?" he gasped.

I didn't respond. I should have said: "She's fine. No problems in that department." But I didn't. I hesitated, and he smiled at me in a knowing way and told me in almost a cavalier fashion how he'd met her after she left me. I was stunned. He laughed as he told me how she'd tracked him down and accused him of having an affair with me.

He leaned forward in his seat, as if that wasn't all. With almost a smile, he looked me straight in the eye and told me my wife had an affair with that policeman I'd been to school with. H said he believed he'd seduced my wife after convincing his bosses he needed to go undercover to gather evidence that I was a drug baron. But, H calmly continued, the policeman went and fell in love with her.

After that last remark, H sat back with a satisfied look on his face and took another big suck on his joint. I could feel him assessing me and he asked me yet again if I'd told her anything. I insisted I hadn't.

H ordered me to go into lockdown with my wife in the cabin, so that I could find out what she'd told that policeman, or anyone else for that matter.

"Don't tell her you know about the affair. Just take your time, old boy, and see what she's really been up to," he said.

When I got in my car after that meeting with H, I had to take some long, deep breaths. My heart was pounding so much.

Of course, I'd suspected it. But now I had to face the reality of what had happened.

* * *

When I got home that afternoon, my wife demanded to know where I'd been. I insisted I'd been to get the car fixed. She seemed not to believe me, and I could have got angry about this (and other things), but I decided I had to try and charm my way through the evening. I also needed to make sure she stayed in my sight at all times and didn't leave.

So once again we sat down and began dismantling our marriage. Sitting across our dining table, I took the blame for all our problems, citing my avoidance of issues and secrecy as bad habits. I knew she'd cheated on me, but it wasn't that surprising she'd slept with someone else, because she thought I had a lover.

The following morning over breakfast, she asked me yet again if I was having an affair, and that was when I felt something inside me snap. She must have seen my face darken as I gritted my teeth. I said nothing.

For the first time, I seriously considered killing her. I imagined how I would do it and what would happen after she died. I didn't do anything, but there it was, in my mind for the first time. The strange thing is that I wasn't in the least bit surprised by my reaction. There was something inevitable about it.

I announced I wasn't going to work because I felt like having a few days off and she looked a bit worried but said nothing. Over the following few days, we hardly spoke. She spent much of her time in her bedroom, where she claimed to be setting up her therapy business. It felt like she was hiding from me.

* * *

They say every marriage needs to be evenly balanced otherwise it will never work. Well, mine had completely tipped in the wrong direction. And in the middle of our current crisis, my therapist wife kept repeating one of her favourite words: empathy. Initially, she used it to refer to how my parents neglected me as a child. But she soon began pointedly rounding on me and my own supposed lack of empathy.

After multiple uses of the dreaded word, I asked her why she kept attacking me when she was the one who'd had the affair. It was the very thing I'd promised H I wouldn't say, but I just couldn't help myself. For once in my life, I'd let my heart rule my head.

She went pale, burst into tears and ran back into the bedroom, slamming the door behind her.

I think one of the keys to surviving life is to work out when to get out of something before it destroys you. How could I have seriously thought I could mend my crumbling marriage while hiding such a massive secret from my wife?

CHAPTER THIRTY-EIGHT
MIXED MESSAGES

She refused to come out of her bedroom for days after I'd confronted her about the policeman. I tried everything to coax her out, but she clearly couldn't face me now that I knew. Unfortunately, I still needed to talk to her properly, so I could find out if either of them knew anything about my business with H. Eventually, I persuaded her to go with me to a nearby waterfall where we could talk in confidence away from the cabin, which was becoming increasingly claustrophobic.

I'd been to Plodda Falls many times as a child. One time, my father hung me upside down from the top of the falls after I kicked him in the shin for being nasty to my mother. The falls themselves were located at the end of a five-mile-long narrow dirt track, which twisted and turned through a dense forest of vast pines that bordered a huge estate, which had, at one time, belonged to one of my father's titled friends.

It was winter and heavy rain was falling so there was no one else there when we arrived. As we walked from where the car was parked into the forest toward the falls, I tried to put my wife at ease by talking about that incident with my father, and suggested we climb up the side of the waterfalls to the exact spot where he'd hung me over the edge.

When we got to where I'd been all those years earlier, I looked down at the water cascading past us and showed her how my father had almost killed me by clambering up onto a boulder right on the edge of the falls. Then I tried to take her hand, so she could join me. She hesitated and for a moment I saw the same look of fear in her eyes as when I told her I was taking some time off work. She quickly changed her mind, though, and took my hand and got up beside me on top of the boulder. We stood there looking down at the rock pool more than 200 feet below.

I told her about how I'd once considered killing myself at this same spot when I was a teenager, soon after my sister and mother had died. She tried not to look surprised and asked me if I still had suicidal thoughts. I said "sometimes" and deliberately left my words hanging in the air. She looked worried, like she thought I might do it there in front of her or – worse still – that I might take her with me. I squeezed her hand reassuringly, but she tried to pull it away, unsure of my intentions.

After a brief discussion, we agreed we had to start really being 100 per cent honest with each other this time. I often wonder how many couples have made that pledge and actually kept to it, but for my wife, it was like turning on a tap inside her head.

She gulped awkwardly and then admitted to her affair. She told me how it had started as a "casual relationship" for them both. He'd chatted her up in a cafe near the college she was attending while training to be a therapist. Then he fell in love with her and persuaded her to leave me for him. She even moved into his flat for a while. I didn't mention to her what H had said about him starting the affair because he'd gone undercover to try and prove I was a drug baron.

She admitted spying on me when I was in the forest on the phone. She insisted she only did it because she thought I was calling my mistress and I believed her. She even revealed how she'd used her policeman lover to track down H's address from the phone number on the text message of the burner phone she'd found before she walked out.

She'd visited H at his cottage and asked him why I'd needed to use a secret phone to talk to him if there was nothing to hide. She said that's when H's mood changed. He told her to be very careful because she was out of her depth. She told me she didn't know what he meant by that but that it had sounded like a warning. As she told me this, I wondered why H hadn't killed her there and then.

I didn't want to hear any more about the confrontation with H because it was making me feel very uncomfortable, as I didn't have any answers to give her. So I asked her about the letter the policeman had sent her about "the car accident".

My wife said they'd had a row and that her lover was distraught that she'd left him and gone back to me. So in desperation he'd sent that official-looking letter to the cabin and followed it up with the contrived visit to us.

After she'd told me everything, we stood there on the boulder with the water cascading past us in silence for at least five minutes.

She pulled her hand away from mine, and suddenly almost lost balance. I grabbed it back and held on tightly to her.

"You don't need to be scared of me," I said quietly.

But she unclasped my hand awkwardly without saying a word, got off the boulder and began walking back toward the car park. I could see she was shaking. I followed her and pleaded with her not to go but she ignored me completely.

"I don't care about the affair," I said. "We can survive that. I know we can."

But she still didn't respond and just carried on walking along the pathway as if I wasn't there. When I tried to stop her again, she brushed me away and warned me not to touch her.

"But we need to talk all this through," I said.

"It's too late for that," she replied flatly.

Her response struck me as sounding very final. I had to do something, so I took a deep breath.

"Stop and listen to me please. I actually have something much more important than all this to tell you."

She stopped on the pathway.

"What?" she asked.

"I am a hitman. There is no mistress. There never has been."

"What are you talking about?" she said, almost dismissively.

"I kill people for a job. That's my secret life. There is no one else."

She looked unsure of what to say.

"You also need to know something else, too," I said.

I told her that her policeman lover had gone undercover to target her deliberately because he thought I was a drug baron. She said she didn't believe me, but I could tell she was very upset. I could see her assessing the information in her head, and gradually it sunk in that it was true. It was only then it occurred to me that we might still have a chance to salvage our marriage.

Looking back, the strangest thing was that she didn't ask me any other questions about being a hitman that day. All the adultery stuff seemed to take priority. Being married to a mass murderer could wait.

We talked about how when we'd originally fallen in love it was like a chemical high but was temporary. When that feeling faded, we'd been left in a dream-like limbo, with a sense of loss about something we never had in the first place.

My wife said: "Love isn't what you feel. It's what you do. You can't go back to the early days of a relationship, to the time before you became angry and disappointed and cut off."

And we'd both lacked the time or the tools to resolve our problems together. I admitted I'd harboured resentment toward her and hated all her accusations. How she was quick to be angry. And those feelings festered for a long time before she left me.

I often think about the mentality and motivation that drives people like me. For a long time, I'd convinced myself that those jobs with H were all about money and kudos. But there was so much more to it than that. Lebanon. My mother. My baby sister. My real father. The list was endless. At the end of the evening, my wife told me I needed to deal with what had driven me to become a contract killer in the first place.

By the time we went to bed, we'd laid more stuff out than we'd probably done throughout our entire marriage.

* * *

I woke up early the next morning and left my wife asleep to go into the kitchen to make some coffee. While I was getting the mugs out, her mobile phone started ringing. She'd left it on a sideboard. On the screen was the name of her policeman friend. He'd rung six times. And there was a text asking her why she hadn't shown up the previous afternoon. He sounded heartbroken.

It seemed I was right. She'd planned to leave me at the falls to be with him.

It was time to make some big decisions.

A few minutes later, I'd just poured myself a coffee when I heard a car approaching. I knew it had to be him. I got to the garden gate just before he reached it and asked him what he wanted. He said he had to speak to my wife. I told him she was asleep.

He ignored me and tried to walk up the path, so I blocked him at the gate and told him about the visit to Plodda Falls and how she'd confessed to her affair with him. He didn't know what to say then. I asked him if this was his way of getting revenge on me for what happened between us when we were kids. He grimaced and repeated that he needed to talk to my wife. He demanded that I get her from the cabin, so he could see her with his own eyes. He warned me that if she had been harmed in any way, he would make sure I paid for it for the rest of my life.

When I questioned what he meant by that, he said she'd told him she was scared of me. I told him to fuck off. I wanted him to try and hit me. But instead he turned and walked away, just like he'd done after I beat him up all those years ago.

* * *

The first few days after the policeman visited the cabin were not easy. We both had a lot of stuff on our minds and recognized that we couldn't just rip into each other because we'd end up going backwards.

The biggest surprise at that time was that I didn't hear another word from H. I eventually tried to contact him, but he'd dumped his mobile phones.

I told my wife and she said I should go and see him to clear the air but warned me to be careful. I didn't tell her I'd already packed my .22.

CHAPTER THIRTY-NINE
CLEAN BREAK

H's cottage looked different as I approached it in my car, but it was only as I got closer that I realized it had been badly damaged in a fire. Half of the roof was missing and the timber beams that held the cottage together were tinged with dark brown burn marks. I got out and looked through the smoke-stained windows and saw that inside it was virtually a burned-out shell. I could just make out a photo of H in a frame that was half burnt and lying face up on the living room carpet.

I was worried where he'd gone and, while I hoped he was okay, I suspected the worst.

When I got back in my car, I found that attitude suddenly hardened. After all, he was the man who probably wanted me and my wife dead. I decided not to try and find him for the time being. This was an opportunity to make a clean break from H, wherever he was.

When I got home, my wife began asking me some very pointed questions about being a hitman. I tried to answer her honestly, but I couldn't include certain details in case anyone found out she knew. She wanted to know who I'd killed and all I told her was that they deserved it. That made her quite angry.

Many questions later, I wriggled out of her interrogation by asking her if she'd seriously contemplated a long-term relationship with the policeman. She admitted she knew about his wife and children, but it was only when I'd told her at the falls how he'd deliberately targeted her in the first place that she'd realized she was doing the wrong thing. Plus, she said this had completely humiliated her.

I eventually got around to asking her if the policeman had ever implied in any way that he knew I was a hitman. She insisted nothing like that ever came up, as they'd both thought I was a drug baron.

She asked me pointedly what H would do if he knew I'd told her everything.

"Nothing," I said.

I think she knew I was lying but chose not to pick me up on it.

It was during these discussions that I saw another side to my wife. She was strong and determined, and actually quite keen to take H on at his own game. She wasn't scared and her priority was to protect me at all costs, despite everything I'd done to her.

I'd been thinking for a while about quitting the cabin because too many people knew about it, and told her that, but she said we shouldn't run away. We stayed there I think because it was the one part of our lives, in all the chaos, that had remained consistent.

Gradually we started to create a more self-sufficient life-style at the cabin. We rarely ventured out and began foraging for a lot of our food from within the forest. I created a new pond to lure in all the aquatic creatures from close by. Meanwhile, my wife increased the size of the vegetable patch and we got some chickens as well.

All this enabled us to have even less involvement with the outside world, except for the occasional shopping trip into town. We studiously avoided our neighbours, who were still 10 miles away. In some ways I'd actually morphed into a peace-loving version of the reclusive ghost that H had once called me. But this ghost was trying his hardest to make amends for what he'd done in the past.

The trouble was that H's fate was bothering me a great deal. I needed to know what had happened to him, then there was a chance I could really walk away from everything and start again. In the back of my mind there was a small nugget of fear that he might still come after us one day. We both knew that if H did ever reappear, he'd most likely make sure we were both permanently silenced. However, all this relied on H still being alive. Since visiting his abandoned, burned-out cottage, I'd become increasingly convinced he had to be dead.

My wife said we needed to find out what had happened to H. Just leaving everything hanging in the air was simply asking for trouble. And of course she was right.

CHAPTER FORTY
GHOST WALKING

I eventually tracked down one of H's old British Army friends, who told me that H was alive, but that his health had taken a nasty turn for the worse. He'd been rescued unconscious from his cottage after a neighbour raised the alarm. Apparently, he'd fallen asleep with a joint in his hand, which had sparked the blaze. H's friend said that the shrapnel still in his brain had been gradually spreading poison throughout his body and affected his stability, which meant he kept falling over. After the fire, H was persuaded to move into a care home for injured soldiers, where he now resided.

I wanted to visit H, but his friend said he was "completely gone" after developing premature Alzheimer's, partially caused by his ever-deteriorating injuries.

Some weeks passed without us hearing another word, and then that same army friend called to tell me that H had died. He'd apparently stepped out of the fourth floor window of his room at the convalescent home and fallen to his death. I found that strange, as he once told me that that was his favourite way to kill when he was in black ops in Northern Ireland.

I wondered if he'd really killed himself or been a victim of a rival hitman. If it was murder, the chances were someone would be coming for us next.

* * *

A few days after this, two men wearing similar dark suits turned up at the cabin in a BMW saloon. My wife and I watched them from the window of our hallway as they got out of their car. We'd talked about this moment ever since I'd found out H was dead.

As they began walking toward the cabin, I grabbed my .22 from the hall table drawer and told her to go into the loft while I dealt with them, but she refused.

When we heard the squeak of the garden gate, I put a finger to my lips and grabbed her hand and we crept up the stairs, out of the sightline of the front door in case they fired into it. They knocked on the front door once, waited and knocked a second and then a third time. As we crouched at the top of the stairs, I heard one of them say, "maybe they're not in".

After a few moments, I noticed both of them in the garden just below the first floor hallway window. They looked up but didn't see us. They moved slowly around the outside of the house, looking through all the ground floor windows, trying to see if anyone was in. I glanced down at them again from the first floor window and noticed they'd walked around almost the entire perimeter of the house.

Moments later, I heard the wooden porch outside the front door creak. But this time they didn't knock. I tightened my grip on my .22 and held my wife's hand for what must have been at least a minute in complete silence.

We heard the front door letter box flip open and snap shut. I glanced down the stairs and noticed a note lying on the floor. I ignored it and we watched them walking back toward their car. We remained sitting on the stairs as the BMW started up and drove off.

I crept down to the hall and checked through the window to make sure both men were in the vehicle as it set off down our drive. I signalled to my wife to come down the stairs.

The note said they were from the Secret Intelligence Service – MI6 – and they needed to speak to me about H. I stood in the hall and read the note twice.

If they'd known who I really was they'd have kicked the front door down and grabbed or most likely shot us. I waited some time before calling the mobile number on their note and asking them to come over for a cup of tea.

The two MI6 officers came back to the house probably as soon as they could have and – after introducing themselves – produced that same photo H kept of us together in the Legion and asked how well I knew him. I said we hadn't spoken since our days in the Legion, except when he came to my father's funeral.

The more talkative one said he was surprised I hadn't seen H more recently because he lived "quite near here".

"We just weren't that close," I replied.

The same one said they were talking to friends and associates of H about the security company he ran before he died.

"Really? What's all that about then?" I asked, trying to sound as if it was news to me.

"We've just started handling a new informant – a well-known London criminal – and he claims your friend ran a company that took commissions for murders."

"Wow. Do such organizations even exist?" I asked.

"Well, our informant assures us that they do. He's also told us that one of your friend's last jobs was to kill him, but that he then paid off the gangsters who'd commissioned the hit on him to ensure he was not killed."

I now realized why my last intended victim near Brighton had his daughter on the back of his Harley-Davidson that day. It must have been a safety measure just in case I still tried to kill him.

I remembered how H had admitted he'd "cocked up" on that job. He'd most likely got so pissed and stoned that he'd forgotten to pull me off the job. And that father and daughter saw my face when they drove past that day.

"These are very heavy characters," explained the other quieter MI6 man, looking right at me as he spoke.

"Our informant told us that the same gangsters then visited your friend at his cottage demanding their money back and the identity of the hitman because they wanted to get rid of him."

I was starting to feel nauseous as I imagined the scene inside that cottage. So I focused my eyeline on a corner of the ceiling and nodded slowly as if I knew nothing about what they were telling me.

"They tortured your friend for hours, but he refused to help them. They took all the cash they could find in the cottage and left him for dead before setting fire to it. It was only thanks to a neighbour that he was rescued alive."

So the story about a dropped joint must have been H's friend's way of protecting H. I sat in silence, still focusing on that same corner of the ceiling.

"You don't seem surprised by any of this?" the less talkative MI6 man asked me.

"I'm just lost for words that my old friend got involved in all this and was nearly killed," I explained.

I asked them where H was now, knowing full well what the answer would be.

"He died recently in a convalescent home," the quieter one said in a very matter-of-fact voice, before his partner took over.

"We believe that those same criminals visited your friend a second time and forced him at gunpoint to jump out of a fourth floor window at that nursing home because he still refused to tell them anything about the hitman."

I noticed the other MI6 man looking straight at me again. "Your friend's loyalty cost him his life."

The more talkative MI6 officer then asked me if I knew anything about someone known as "the ghost", whom he described as "the hitman who apparently worked with your friend".

I said I'd never heard of such a person.

"Well," said the quieter MI6 man. "I hope he's somewhere safe, because those criminals will kill him if they ever find him."

They stood up, thanked us for the cup of tea and left. As my wife and I watched them get into their car and drive off, I felt even more nauseous and ran to the bathroom and vomited.

I'd been totally wrong about H and I felt as if I'd cost him his life. It was a similar feeling to what happened after I killed that child in the Lebanon. Yet even though I did owe H everything, there was another side to me that was still relieved that he was dead. I could never even contemplate starting a new life if he was still around.

And there was another problem. That MI6 informant and his daughter had briefly caught a glimpse of me at the hit site near Brighton after I'd managed to cut the wire across the country lane. I kept wondering why the MI6 officers hadn't mentioned that, unless their informant had chosen not to tell them.

The following afternoon my wife drove into the nearest town for some provisions and I decided it was time to go into the forest and finally dig up the biggest secret of all.

CHAPTER FORTY-ONE
LIFE INSURANCE

A few minutes after my wife drove off, I headed out of the cabin. It was snowing hard and all the forest's familiar sounds were even more muffled than usual. Despite the winter light fading fast and the snow covering the ground, I still managed to spot the two small logs I'd left earlier leaning against a tree trunk. Seeing those, I knew I was going in the right direction.

I eventually reached a narrow stream rippling in the fading light as it twisted and turned through the thick foliage, banked with snow. As I followed the stream by walking along its bank, I thought I heard the sound of twigs snapping behind me. If someone was out there watching me, there were certainly enough contenders – from all of my victims to the criminals to the security services of at least three nations. But the gangsters the MI6 men had told me about were probably the most likely ones to be out there if anyone was. Maybe the MI6 informant had told them he saw me in that country lane after all.

I looked up tentatively, trying to make sure that whoever was there would not know I'd heard them. The light had faded and I couldn't see anyone. So I continued on. My torch guided me through the soggy bracken in the direction of a rickety plank, which crossed the stream to my left. I walked hesitantly across it because it was so hard to see my footing in the darkness. I moved over slippery mounds of moss and fallen logs to where a tall, thin pine tree majestically shot up toward the black sky. I fell to my knees in front of the trunk and pulled a small hand shovel out of my backpack and began digging.

Moments later I heard the muffled sound of broken bracken and twigs underfoot again. I ignored it at first and carried on digging, so whoever was there would think I hadn't noticed them. If it was those gangsters from the Brighton job, they would have killed me by now. I looked back in the direction of those sounds. Nobody seemed to be there. I thought it must just be my paranoia, so I carried on.

I kept digging and eventually pulled out the large plastic container that contained the metal box. Inside it were tens of thousands of pounds wrapped in see-through plastic. But beneath that money was something much more important; dozens of neatly stacked mini audio cassettes in see-through plastic boxes wrapped together in clingfilm.

This was the secret that would ensure that if anything ever happened to us then my crimes and those who commissioned them would be exposed to the world. This was my buried treasure. It was more valuable than all the money I'd earned in the killing game. I'd secretly recorded virtually everything I'd ever done. Many of my numerous chats with H. Every job, including most of the kills themselves. No one knew about those tapes except me and they had the potential to bring a lot of people down if I ever got caught. I could use them to bargain my way out, whether by fear or coercion, with the good guys or the bad ones. I also hoped I could use them to protect my wife.

If someone was out there watching me and about to pounce, I'd just led them straight to the evidence that was keeping us safe.

Then I heard another noise. It was much closer this time. I swung my torch in the direction it came from and my beam of light illuminated the person who was following me.

It was my wife.

"What are you doing?" she asked suspiciously.

"Making sure there will be no more secrets between us," I replied.

Then we took all the audio tapes back to the cabin.

* * *

Later on, we sat with a piping hot cup of tea each in front of a raging fire and I told her how I'd first secretly taped my parents when I was a child because I liked to play back their voices when I was alone at night in my bedroom. I would never have taped my career as a hitman if it hadn't been for what had happened when I was growing up.

At first, my wife was virtually lost for words at what I'd produced from that hole in the forest. So I explained the significance of the recordings and how important they were for our future.

"Did you secretly record us as well?" she asked.

I smiled as she waited for my reaction. For a few moments, she looked as serious as she had during the worst of our marriage problems. Then I assured her I had not. She said it was a nice feeling to know for the first time in years that I wasn't lying.

Later, my wife was in the kitchen cooking supper while I looked down at all the tapes in front of me and thought about the worst parts of my life, which they represented. I wondered if it had all been worth it. Maybe, I thought to myself, I should just burn them all and then we'd never have to deal with the fallout from the tapes. There was no point in having them if no one knew about them. I was desperately looking for answers that night and, in the process, I found myself deeply regretting everything I'd done. I took one of the mini cassettes out of its box and gripped it with a pair of fire tongs and held it over the open fire and watched it start to curl with the heat.

As my wife walked in from the kitchen and saw what I was doing, she ordered me to stop immediately. She said the tapes were part of both of us now and she wouldn't let me destroy them. She reiterated that as long as we had them, we were safe. The key, if anything, was that no one else knew they existed.

That made them our secret trump card. No one could hurt us thanks to them.

* * *

When it comes to my marriage, all I can say is that, even though it was never going to be an easy ride, it was worth everything to save it.

After we got back together, we went through all the same stages as most couples who reconcile. There was a rush of happiness and excitement after we started over again. That was followed by a lot of unanswered questions from both sides. This sparked moments of great intensity and a lot of tears. And there was the whole question of trust.

In the end, we both concluded that we were guilty as charged in that department, and we had to accept that the trust issues had cancelled each other out, in a sense.

* * *

Eventually my wife got pregnant again and the paediatrician assured us it would be okay this time.

I no longer had the albatross of H and the killing business round my neck. Our lives were simple and uncomplicated, and my wife even commented on how happy the news seemed to have made me this time round.

With a baby on the way, I decided it was time to retrieve all the cash I'd hidden in those forest stashes while I was working with H. I also had a lot of money from my foss business, which I'd just sold for a healthy profit to a German hedge fund.

I used some of that cash to buy back my father's old house and renovate it. My wife tried to dissuade me at first. She thought we needed to make a clean break of it. I believed that moving back into that mansion was a way to reconnect with my mother and baby sister. There was also an entire wing which my wife could turn into her therapy clinic. When I said that, she immediately agreed.

I did make sure not to sink all my cash into that house, though. I'd been secretly sending a large donation every year to the family of that child I killed on the stairway ever since my first job for H, and I wanted to continue. Paying out that money didn't excuse what I'd done to that family, but at least it meant I could show them that their son would never be forgotten.

My life felt strangely empty without H on the other end of a phone line or rolling a joint with his feet up on the desk in his small, untidy cottage. Ultimately, he'd remained a true, loyal friend right to the end of his life. More than can be said of me.

I'd now settled for a simple life and I was so grateful to my wife for sticking by me. Then along came the baby. That was challenging and exciting and it was also mundane, in a healthy sort of way.

No matter whatever else was going on in my life, I still thought a lot about that double life I once led. It was dangerous, reckless and extremely destructive (to say the least), but it was fucking exciting.

Over the years, there were times when I felt the power I used to have. One time a property developer bought some of the land next to our house and tried to build an apartment block on the edge of my favourite forest. I went round to him and convinced him to abandon his plans with some "friendly suggestions".

So I know I'm still capable of being dangerous. How could I not be after killing all those people? I can't just wake up one morning and wipe the slate clean. It's inside you for ever.

I hope I can now say – hand on heart – I would never kill another human being. Whenever that old feeling kicks in, the new me steps up to the plate and sees sense. That's when little things in life hit the spot; just saying hello to a stranger in the street is weirdly uplifting after what I've been through.

Throughout all this, my affinity toward my favourite forest has never wavered. Most mornings I still walk out into it either alone or with my wife. There are no more secretive phone calls to H and the stash holes have been carefully filled in, but I still often get lost in my thoughts in that forest. Sometimes just being there makes it harder for me to even relate to the reality of what I've actually done. At moments like that, it feels lik

I was nothing more than an observer watching all that death and destruction without actually having taken part in it.

I do know that my wife and I would never have stayed together if I'd continued to keep my secrets from her. Some will no doubt say I was selfish to unload everything on her and presume she would keep it from the outside world. It's almost as if I pushed the responsibility onto her, but that's not the way I look at it.

The funny thing is that she sometimes makes jokes about my life as a hitman and how if I don't clean the dishes she might get me killed. I find those moments very reassuring.

AFTERTHOUGHTS

It's still possible I'll one day disappear for ever. Someone may well come and get me. Let's face it; there's a long line of potential enemies out there, from the spy services of at least three nations to the organized crime kings whose operations I could expose, not to mention many others.

Paranoia drives most things in what was once my line of business. Hopefully that means that while I might think someone is out there ready to pounce, most of that is only down to what's in my head.

H and I thought we'd kept everything secret, although it didn't turn out that way in the end. I hope I managed to stay one step ahead of anyone who might be after me. And we have those audio tapes which should guarantee that myself and my wife can stay safe.

I made many promises to my wife after we fully reconciled. The biggest one of all was that I would never seek revenge on that policeman who tried to steal her from me. I heard he moved back in with his wife and two children and eventually got a new posting to a large Scottish city, where he ended u running the CID. I wish him good luck, and I mean it. I really do, because if he hadn't come along when he did my marriage would have collapsed completely and I'd still be killing for a living or someone would have put me in an early grave.

It's taken me a long time to work out why I thought I had the right to decide if someone lived or died. There's no getting away from the fact I'd become a deadly, cold-blooded killing machine. I thrived in a secret netherworld of crime and retribution. Somehow I'd thought it was okay to be a devoted husband and a murderous criminal all at the same time. But my licence to hurt other people has now hopefully expired. I'm not sure I'll ever know why I felt so compelled to do this when it was so obviously immoral.

My story is intended to be much more than just another criminal telling all in the hope of some form of retribution. I've tried my hardest to say something new about a secret netherworld that needed to be properly exposed from the inside looking out.

I worried that the chaos, death and destruction described here would be too much for many people to absorb. I thought I'd end up sending some readers heading for the hills in search of something lighter and more uplifting. Who knows, maybe I have.

One day I'll write a follow-up to this book *if* it sells enough copies. The new one would be a lot more gentle and called

"*The Man Who Came Back Down to Earth With a Bump – How a Typical Yuppie Baby Boomer Learned to Appreciate Animals and Life.*" Because that's how my life has evolved, now I've got so much off my chest.

Being a hitman enabled me to experience all that danger in order to build up the confidence to get on to the next part of my life. That's not to say I don't think about *all* my victims every day of my life. Not just those from each job, but also my mother, my baby sister and that boy in the stairwell. I've been trying for virtually a lifetime to come to terms with what happened to them. No one – including me – has the right to say who is good and who is bad, and who deserves to die and who doesn't. My professional victims were all husbands, sons and brothers as well.

My wife's tried very hard to make me understand that such thoughts can have a huge impact on your life. Her training as a therapist has obviously helped give her a special insight. She said I was not the baddest person in the world. There were always others who'd done worse than me. She told me I was locked in a prison that I'd built for myself.

I was trapped in my own mind. My thoughts and beliefs determined how I felt, what I did and what I thought was possible. My wife helped me realize I could change. But in order to do so, I had to be aware of my own suffering as well as that of others. As long as I retained my curiosity about what would happen next, then I would stay on the right path.

I'd had to walk away from my job after that last hit went wrong. The child on the motorbike triggered something inside me that had been trying to shape me since childhood. If it hadn't taken so long to come out, maybe a lot of lives would not have been lost.

If this had been a Hollywood blockbuster, I, the bad guy, would have had to die at the end, because that's the way the movies like it. The trouble with that "rule" is that stories like mine would never have been told if I'd already been "taken care of". In the real world, you don't get to choose who lives and dies. Well, I did in a sense, but I still didn't get to make that choice when it really mattered.

No doubt some will say disparagingly that I took to killing like, in someone else's words, "a fat fly to dog shit". Yet here I still am in one piece, which is a miracle in itself. Ultimately, my life as a hitman gave me a chance to overachieve, to prove myself.

I didn't pass many exams at school and yet I managed to fulfil all my dreams: a beautiful home, a wonderful wife and child. I don't deserve it after what I've done.

If my life ended tomorrow it wouldn't be that big a deal. Maybe I've accepted it. A lot of people claim they're not afraid of dying without fully appreciating the finality of what they're saying. No one *really* wants to die. They say they do but when the grim reaper is lurking on your shoulder, most will do everything in their power to shake him off. But I feel utterly unafraid because I know how lucky I am to have even got this far.

I know it's a foregone conclusion that I'm going to hell, whatever that means. Perhaps joining the devil downstairs might not be so bad after all. Hell sounds like a place where all the inhabitants are much more equal than heaven. All those who go there have done such bad things that we all start on the same level. Anyway, I would suspect hell is also the place where most of my professional hit victims will now be residing, so I suppose I should be a bit careful what I wish for. If they all gang up on me, it might not be much fun for me. But it's no more than I deserve. I do have one regret about going to hell, though. My mother, baby sister and that child in the Lebanon will have gone to heaven and it would have been nice to have met them again.

Ultimately, I don't want people to read my story and think: "There's no way my problems stack up with his." I want people to read my story and think: "If he can start again, so can I!" I've turned all those lessons I've learned into a gift for everyone who reads this book. This is an opportunity to decide what kind of life you want and free yourself from anything that's holding you back. Change is synonymous with growth. I have to evolve instead of revolve. I studied Latin at that expensive boarding school and there was one phrase that always stuck in my mind: *Tempora mutantur, nos et mutamur in illis* (Times are changing, and we are changing with them).

So despite everything, I believe that my graphic, often chilling story has one upbeat message. If I can reach this stage of my life still in one piece, there is hope for us all.

I want this story to end neatly, with an arc. Maybe that's why this book exists. At the start of all this, I sung the praises of secrets and how they empower you. Now I recognize I was utterly wrong. Keeping secrets tainted my entire life until recently, and I would now say to anyone who is keeping one deep inside them that they need to give it up. Send it on its way because it will only cause untold destruction to your life and those around you if you keep hiding it from the world. And the damage wrought by my obsession with having secrets is undeniable.

DEDICATION

My wife is at the centre of this story, so therefore it is only right that I dedicate this book to her. I didn't do it at the beginning because I didn't want to give anything away.

Without her, I'm certain my reckless nature would have cost me either my life or my liberty by now. I need her steadiness and good heart to counterbalance the madness of my life more than ever.

Thank God I told her my biggest secret before writing my story, because she would have soon worked out where all this came from when she read it and that would have been the end of us.

My wife has patiently coaxed so much out of me without making me feel I am the most evil man in the world. That was clever, because people never open up if they feel bad about themselves.

Today, I realize secrets spread a poisonous venom through your mind which is hard to shake off. They distort the truth, making it seem better to lie than be honest.

I finally got around to asking my wife the other day if I had given the game away when I was having all those nightmares. She smiled and said: "Of course not. If I'd known you were a hitman back then I would have got you arrested."

Not long ago, my wife and I were watching a true crime TV documentary together about a serial killer. We no longer have any of those awkward silences that used to happen in front of the television during our marriage problems. But she did say one odd thing about how I was, in a sense, a serial killer myself. She bluntly pointed out that I'd cold-bloodedly murdered complete strangers and those victims had no direct connection to each other, which is the official definition of a serial killer after all. My defence has always been that they deserved to die. But after I retired, my wife made me appreciate that that was an empty excuse for what I've done. In some cases, there wasn't even any proof that my victims had killed anyone else. I'd conveniently ignored that.

Those are the rare moments when I wonder if my wife would ever turn on me and help the police to bring me to justice. But those thoughts usually only last a few seconds, like that time before when I did once consider killing her.

So here we are still together despite that sword of Damocles hanging over me. I need it there because in a typical, twisted way, I want to be prevented from stepping out of line as I cannot afford to be what I was before.

AUTHOR'S ENDNOTE

It was never the intention of this book to ever bring anyone down. Those who feared my disclosures when they first heard about what I had done can rest easy and hopefully let me get on with the rest of my life.

Many who've read my story will no doubt wonder how it was possible for me to recall so many detailed (albeit carefully disguised) conversations. I had those audio tapes and my wife transcribed them all after she had our baby. That's how I was able to provide such specific dialogue involving myself and many of the other characters featured here.

Just to reiterate, the salient details of my life you've read here are not always 100 per cent accurate. All memories are clouded by time and emotions, so it's possible that sometimes I've veered into territory that might not completely tally with the facts.

Some very dangerous people are going to be studying every word of my story looking for any clues that might lead to them. I'm now satisfied that nothing here will irk them and I hope they'd agree that now is the best time to let the dust settle.

I could have gone back to some of those who played a role in my life story to verify certain material, but most are no longer with us and the rest would not have appreciated having a starring role in my life story.

I'm going to disappear back into my favourite forest soon, but I wanted to make sure this book had first been completed to everyone's satisfaction.

Putting my story down on paper has never been about money. It's about closure. The only way I can continue building the next chapter of my life is to end the last one first. Hopefully this book will enable me to find some peace for the rest of my life, even though I'll always be looking over my shoulder, just in case there is someone there.

"It takes a certain kind of person to be able to kill another human being."

– Glennon Engleman, American hitman.